The Practitioner Inqu

Marilyn Cochran-Smith and Susan]

(continued)

Reading Families

The Literate Lives
of
Urban Children

CATHERINE COMPTON-LILLY

FOREWORD BY
BARBARA COMBER

Teachers College
Columbia University
New York and London

Published by Teachers College Press, 1234 Amsterdam Avenue, New York, NY 10027

Author's notes:
Sections of Chapters 3 and 4 were previously published in an article by Catherine Compton-Lilly entitled "Staying on Children: Challenging Stereotypes About Urban Parents," which appeared in *Language Arts*, copyright 2000 by the National Council of Teachers of English. Reprinted with permission.

Chapter 6 was previously published as an article for the online teacher research journal *Networks*. *Networks* can be viewed at www.oise.utoronto.ca/~ctd/networks.

This research was supported in part by a grant from the Genesee Valley Developmental Learning Group.

Library of Congress Cataloging-in-Publication Data

Compton-Lilly, Catherine.
 Reading families : the literate lives of urban children / Catherine Compton-Lilly ; foreword by Barbara Comber.
  p. cm. — (The practitioner inquiry series)
  Includes bibliographical references and index.
  ISBN 0-8077-4276-7 (pbk. : alk. paper) — ISBN 0-8077-4277-5 (cloth : alk. paper)
  1. City children–Education–United States–Case Studies. 2. City children–Books and reading–United States–Case Studies. 3. Reading–Parent participation–United States–Case studies. 4. Education, Urban–United States–Case Studies. I. Title. II. Series.

 LC5131 .C615 2002
 372.42'5—dc21   2002028502

ISBN 0-8077-4276-7 (paper)
ISBN 0-8077-4277-5 (cloth)

Printed on acid-free paper

Manufactured in the United States of America

10 09 08 07 06 05 04 03   8 7 6 5 4 3 2

DEDICATION

This book is dedicated to the poets in my life—

> Hearts glistening in the sky,
> Erasing hate by love,
> Apart, never together, always,
> Racing, dashing from heart to heart.
> Tonight loves soars into your heart.
> —C.C.L., age 8

> The voices that were never supposed to be:
> Scrawled this on the station wall:
> Nobody wanted to ride it anyway.
>
> We knew it when we
> Made the valleys high
> And laid the mountains low
> To make the grade at the river bridge;
>
> Then gain speed
> Passing tired factories and
> Clapboard houses that
> Were never meant to be passed down.
>
> And at the crossing
> The children lean on their dreams and wonder:
> "What a strange sight,
> Who'd build such a thing
> Without asking?"
>
> While inside the carriages
> The empty berths sway and
> Clank in florescent light
> And perpetual hope.
>
> Everyone likes the thought of a train
> Whistling its way across the night.
> —T.K.L., age 48

Contents

Foreword

Teachers cannot control children's lives out of school. As much as they might wish them to be different—happier, healthier, wealthier—children's home environment is subject to wider forces, such as the way society distributes its resources and the extent to which families are able to access those resources. Teachers, however, can make a great deal of difference to children's lives within schools. Understanding and recognizing children's capacities and potential is crucial. We know that when teachers subscribe to deficit views of what specific groups of children can achieve, their underestimation can do irrevocable damage and impede educational trajectories. We know also that when teachers recognize that all their students possess potential and respect their families' cultural and linguistic practices, their high expectations have a positive impact on children's learning. The last decade has been marked with a so-called "literacy crises" in many nations, with admonitions to address falling standards and invest huge sums of money on literacy testing. At the same time, the gaps between the rich and poor have widened. Catherine Compton-Lilly's book is indeed very welcome at this time. Her interviewees are the parents and grandparents of children in her classroom. She invites us to listen to the families of children in an urban neighborhood, to listen to what they make of reading in their daily lives and what they want for their children.

Reading Families: The Literate Lives of Urban Children is an important book by a teacher-researcher firmly committed to social justice. Compton-Lilly disrupts deficit discourses about the educational aspirations of families living in urban poverty. She tackles head-on the dangerous and incorrect assumptions that circulate about poor parents' supposed lack of concern for their children's education. Through her research with families, she discovers and demonstrates that parents and grandparents living in poverty do engage in a complex and varied range of reading practices. She also explores the limits and potentials of literate practices to make a material difference in the lives of socio-economically struggling families.

What is most striking about Compton-Lilly's approach is that she sets out to listen to learn from her students' families. We can hope that many other teachers will be inspired by this work and take another look in their neighborhoods and listen to community members. Compton-Lilly really listens to what these parents and grandparents have to say and reports it without romantic storytelling or white middle-class overlays. The way she positioned her informants to provide a local analysis of reading in their lives is a lesson in itself. The book introduces powerful new vocabularies for thinking about the ways these parents and grandparents provide educational support for the children in their care, including developing a sense of tenacity and stubbornness. These families "stay on" their young people: that is, they emphasize the need to work at school, to struggle with challenging ideas, to learn to read. Compton-Lilly opens our eyes to the work they do and gives us new interpretive resources for appreciating practices which often go discounted.

In its respect for impoverished and culturally diverse families this book is reminiscent of work by Shirley Brice Heath, Bob Connell, and Anne Haas Dyson. Because it was produced by a teacher-researcher working in her own context, it offers something different in that very few educators deliberately contest the pervasive and harmful idea that the poor are to blame for their poverty and that education (and indeed literacy) is the solution. Compton-Lilly locates her work in the tradition of socio-political and socio-cultural approaches to literacy. Her interpretations are strengthened by a particularly revealing combination of ethnographic research and critical discourse analysis. Through her scholarship and intense respect for the families who informed this study, we have access to different ways of thinking about the reading practices of urban families and their implications for classroom teaching.

Reading Families: The Literate Lives of Urban Children raises some new questions for literacy researchers and educators about how alienation from schooling is produced. Compton-Lilly's observations about the physicality and sociality associated with reading redirect us to consider what counts for people in literate practices. This is a brave and scholarly book by a teacher-researcher who dares to listen to the insights of her parent community. It sets new standards for those us committed to social justice through literacy education.

Barbara Comber
Centre for Studies in
Literacy Policy and Learning Cultures
University of South Australia

Acknowledgments

Despite the single name printed on the cover of this book, writing is a social practice and many people have been involved in the conception and creation of this book. I have been extremely fortunate to be surrounded by colleagues, friends, and family members who have taken an interest in my professional work and who have supported me through both the research and the writing processes.

I would first like to thank the members of my dissertation committee: David Hursh, Joanne Larson, Patricia Irving, and Jane Hogan. Your thoughts, ideas, input, and guidance were critical to the development of this book.

Carole Edelsky, Patrick Shannon, Marjorie Siegel, Gerald Coles, Susan Goodwin, Susan Novinger, Robert Compton, and Doug Noble provided valuable responses to drafts of chapters and never failed to encourage me as I wrote and rewrote sections of this book. I would also like to thank Sue Constable and Kathy Broikou for your support and interest in my work. I could not ask for better colleagues.

A small grant from the Genesee Valley Developmental Group helped to offset some of the costs of this research; and three additional Teacher Research Grants from the International Reading Association, the National Council of Teachers of English, and the Rochester Teacher Center are enabling me to continue working with the families presented in this book now that my former students are in fifth grade. This financial support has been extremely helpful.

I would like to thank the editorial staff at Teachers College Press, particularly Carol Collins and Amy Kline. The reviews from three anonymous reviewers were extremely helpful in expanding my thinking and focusing my thoughts.

Perhaps the most important people to thank are the generous parents and children who have spent many hours talking to me about their experiences and their lives. They have taught me many valuable lessons about teaching and I am greatly indebted to them. I look forward to continuing to work with each of them as my former students continue through school.

Finally, I want to thank Todd and Carly, who have put up with my absence on countless mornings and evenings as first a dissertation and then a book came to be. You are both at the center of my world and my two best friends. Thank you.

Introduction

When I asked the parents of my urban first-grade students why it was important that their children learn to read, their answers did not focus on reading for success in school. Rather, the parents of my students spoke about the importance of reading in the lives of their children.

> *Ms. Holt:* In order to go from place to place you have to know how to read—stop signs, road signs. What building is this? You have to know how to read. If you can't read, you can't go no places. . . . Where is so and so? They'll point at it and you can't read it because normally the sign say City Hall or Burger King or McDonalds. You have to be able to read that.

> *Ms. Johnson:* You have to be able to read you know in the grocery store [to know] what you're buying. You have to know. Even when you go to the bank. You have to know what accounts [you have]. You have to know, to read all that stuff. You know there's a lot of important things you have to know how to read [such as] your mail.

> *Ms. Rodriguez:* To make it in this world you're going to have to read. Even if you are going to the store or the corner, you got to know where you at.

Parents clearly understand that learning to read involves the ability to participate in a range of real-life activities that entail reading.

Like others in our society, children in urban communities see people reading in their daily lives and they are exposed to written language in a variety of forms and in a range of settings. Environmental print is everywhere in their urban neighborhood. By the time they arrive in my first-grade classroom, many students are already beginning to master basic understandings about how print operates and how it can be deciphered. Thus, children do not enter my school as blank slates; they have experienced reading and its effects in many ways. Prior experiences with reading; the experiences of siblings, peers, and parents; and the role reading has played in the lives of their parents and grandparents each play a role in the construction of my students' attitudes and identities as readers.

Most students enter my classroom from poor urban homes. Many of their families suffer unemployment and underemployment as they struggle to withstand the economic and social pressures of living in an urban community. My students live in a particular neighborhood, attend a particular school, and deal with particular obstacles in their lives. Unfortunately, based on the situations in which many children live, assumptions are often made about the quality and quantity of the reading experiences they bring to school. Assumptions are made about children's families, their reading habits, and their reading abilities, while teachers rarely take the opportunity to learn about the actual reading lives of their students and their students' families. The major goal of this research is to document the ways my students and their parents view reading and to situate their experiences within the social and political world they inhabit.

In order to understand reading as a cultural practice, it is essential that we consider the social relationships and political positioning that accompany the experience of learning to read in this urban school. Before we can begin to understand the ways urban students and their parents conceptualize reading, let us first consider the ways urban parents are represented and portrayed. Teachers complain that the parents do not care about their children's education, much less their children as readers.

> I have a problem being evaluated by parents who are not accepting their responsibilities. This year there was about 80 percent parent involvement at fall conferences, 25 percent involvement at open house. Fifteen percent of the class was absent 35–95 days; 10 percent were tardy upward of 37 times; 60 percent of parents came for spring conferences (mandatory); 20 percent of students didn't come the last day of school to get their report card or summer work packet.
>
> Editorial, written by a teacher in my school district

Parents often appear to be the logical culprit for the difficulties children face in school, but negative attitudes about urban parents reach beyond teachers.

> In the past few years, the education of our children nationwide has been severely criticized. The blame has been widespread: unqualified teachers, poor facilities, attitude of students, TV, apathy of parents, etc.

It seems to me that a recent survey pinpointed the problem, at least to a large extent. The survey listed the following high schools [three local suburban districts are listed] as doing a very fine job. Are their teachers better trained? I doubt it.

The logical conclusion is that the parents in these school districts are very intelligent and better educated in general. Thus they are more likely to be more responsive to the needs of their children which enhances the attitude and abilities of these students.

Editorial, written by a local resident

These comments are not unusual. We hear and read them all the time in reference to urban students; "The parents of those kids . . . " and the rest of the sentence is completed with "don't care," "can't read," "don't read," or some other judgment based on the perceived incompetence of urban parents. These myths that blame and berate urban families are pervasive in our society. Media representations of poor urban families and urban issues contribute to the dissemination and acceptance of negative assumptions about urban families within the larger society.

In this Introduction, I will focus on the lessons I learned as a teacher-researcher and the assumptions I had made as an urban first-grade teacher. This book will contribute to a growing body of work (Heath, 1983; Moll, Amanti, Neff, & Gonzalez, 1992; Nieto, 1996; Purcell-Gates, 1995; Shockley, Michalove, & Allen, 1995; Taylor & Dorsey-Gaines, 1988) that challenges stereotypes about urban families and portrays urban families as interested and engaged in the literacy development of their children. The names of all children, parents, and educators mentioned in this book have been changed.

Although I had considered myself a teacher who did not judge parents and had actively resisted "parent bashing" sessions in the teachers' room, becoming a teacher-researcher and interviewing my first-grade students and their parents enabled me to recognize some of my own biases; thus, I cannot claim to be on any higher moral ground than my peers. Allow me to share three stories that occurred early in the research process.

My first step in beginning this research project was to locate 10 parents of children in my class who would be willing to participate in a series of interviews. I remember my apprehension as I reviewed my class list. Whom should I call first? What would these parents say to me? Would they be interested in helping me with this project? I considered calling parents whom I knew fairly well or parents I suspected might be willing to help, but I dismissed this idea because I wanted a random sample. Finally, I decided to start at the top of my alphabetized class list and contact parents until I had 10 parents who were willing to be interviewed. I was amazed and relieved. Every parent I contacted, except one, agreed to be interviewed; parents without telephones were contacted personally. The one parent who did not agree explained that she was due to have a baby the following week but would be happy to help if I called back in a month. Thus, some of my assumptions about urban parents were squelched even before the interviews began. Urban parents are interested in their children's education and willing to go beyond typical school expectations.

Once the interviews began, more assumptions began to crumble. When I walked into Alisa's home, there was little furniture, only a ragged sofa and a small television set perched on an old wobbly table. The hardwood floor was painted a dark brown but the room was clean, and sunshine streamed in the front window. Alisa's mom, Ms. Rodriguez, greeted me at the door. We immediately fell into our familiar parent-teacher friendship. Alisa's brother had been in my class several years before and was one of the best readers I had ever taught. As soon as I sat down, Alisa's mother sent her son to get a box from the back room. He dragged the heavy box across the floor. Inside were hundreds of books. I recognized Little Golden Books, board books, Dr. Seuss books, textbooks, and used books bought form the library. Ms. Rodriguez explained that she had been collecting books for her family since the birth of her first son, who is now graduating from high school. She described going to garage and library sales to collect old books. She reported that there was a second box in the back room. Even the poorest homes I entered had books available for their children to read.

Finally, I learned that within my 10 focus families, two of my students had grandmothers who had been teachers. Often teachers in urban schools tend to distance themselves from the families of their students. We live in neighborhoods removed from the school community, we view ourselves as belonging to a different social class, and we are often members of different ethnic or racial groups. Despite these differences, the grandparents of two of my students were teachers. Prior to this research project, I had never considered the possibility that my daughter and her children could someday be living in an inner-city neighborhood and that my grandchildren might attend schools like the one in which I taught.

Throughout the interviews and over the course of a year, the families I worked with constantly reinforced these early lessons. In contrast to the stereotypes of urban parents that portray them as unconcerned about their children's academic progress, the parents I interviewed taught me otherwise. Parents consistently expressed their strong beliefs about the importance of reading in their children's lives, and no parent ever questioned the value and importance of reading; parents felt that reading was among the things children needed for "survival." Ms. Horner's comments are typical; "Yeah, um, I think of read[ing] as uh, uh, a daily function. You need to learn. You need to be able to read in order to survive. It's definitely important." Ms. Johnson's husband has very limited reading skills. She has learned firsthand the challenges that accompany not being able to read.

> Everything he [her son] will ever do in his life he has to read. I mean there is reading in no matter what you do. You fill out an application for a job you have to read. You have to read the paper. I mean everything you do. I mean especially if you have a job that requires that. I mean you have to read to understand. And then if you can't read, you miss out on a lot.

These parents clearly value reading and want their children to become competent readers. However, as my colleagues so often respond, "Just because parents say they value reading that doesn't mean that they help their children at home." The parents describe myriad ways in which they help their children learn to read. They describe assisting children with reading, monitoring and checking their homework, showing an interest in their children's efforts, having children watch educational television shows, helping children find books they like, reading to children, spelling words for children, reading signs while traveling in the car, taking children to the library, talking to children about what they read, and purchasing books, flashcards, educational toys, computers, and other supplies for children.

Finally, the most powerful lesson I learned about parents in my school community concerns the remarkable degree of resilience they display in their daily lives. I often found myself in awe of their dedication and diligence despite overwhelming odds. During the 9 months in which I interviewed students and parents, the 10 families I interviewed experienced many setbacks, including a father's relapse with cancer, the recent death of a teenage son, a teenage pregnancy, the amputation of both legs suffered by a live-in boyfriend, eviction from a condemned apartment, and a special education student being "pushed out" (Fine, 1991) of high school in May of his senior year with no reasons offered to the family. These setbacks were in addition to the daily stresses of urban life faced by urban families.

This book explores how generally accepted discourses concerning the use of literacy and the possibilities created through literacy learning operate within a community in which many families have been denied access to mainstream ways of life that many people take for granted (safe communities, homes that meet safety codes, jobs that provide a living wage, healthy diets, adequate educational experiences). Discourses identify people as belonging to particular social groups and entail socially defined ways of speaking, thinking, acting, and believing. In this book I apply discourse analysis—analysis of syntactical, pragmatic, and lexical aspects of texts—to the words of my students and their parents. Specifically, I explore the ways mainstream discourses, generally accepted ways of viewing the world, position my students and their families and how alternative ways of viewing the world intersect with these mainstream discourses.

Despite setbacks, a majority of the parents in this study had completed or were in the process of completing degrees and certifications beyond their high school diploma. These parents believe that education will lead to better employment opportunities and a better life. I was deeply impressed by the idea that parents could work, raise children, and go to school without the monetary assets and conveniences that I rely upon (quality child care, reliable transportation, and fast food).

EXPLORING THE DISCOURSES THAT OCCUPY SCHOOLS

At our first interview, Jasmine's mother and I sat at the kitchen table. I asked her why it was important that Jasmine learned to read. She responded:

> Because she has to know places to go or places or anything, anything you need to do is always reading, instructions, anything. Anything is mostly reading. Signs, you need to learn [to read] them. It is really important to learn to read because there is a lot of things you need to know for you to read. If you don't know how to read then you are not going to get nowhere. You're not going to know how to do this and you're not going to know how to do that.

Jasmine and her family live in the complex of housing projects that surrounds my school. Contrary to the assumptions often made about urban parents, Jasmine's mother is adamant about the importance of her daughter's learning to read. Her comments are spoken with passion. Her choice of words (*anything, always,* and *really*) emphasizes the importance of her message and the disastrous results of not knowing how to read.

However, the teachers and administrators at my school, like the teachers quoted earlier, complain that the parents do not care about reading or support their children as readers. When I describe parents such as Jasmine's mother to my colleagues, they dismiss my data, insisting that while parents may say they are concerned, they really are not, or that the parents of their students are not like mine. My colleagues cite the low academic progress of students in my school as evidence of the parents' lack of interest in their children as readers.

Unfortunately, the voices of educators as they blame and berate urban parents are not aberrations; they reflect mainstream discourses that are typically invoked to describe poor, urban residents. My colleagues do not speak in an evil or mean-spirited manner; they are hardworking teachers who are deeply concerned about their students. Their words reflect our culture. The news media, politicians, and economists often portray urban communities as deficit, dangerous, violent, and drug-infested.

Norman Fairclough explains that adopting particular discourses is part of the socialization process of becoming a teacher, in that

> to become a teacher, one must master the discursive and ideological norms which the school attaches to that subject position—one must learn to talk like a teacher and "see things" (i.e., things such as learning and teaching) like a teacher. (1995, p. 39)

The concept of discourses is useful for beginning to understand the ways teachers, parents and children construct their understandings of themselves and their worlds. James Paul Gee uses *Discourse* with the upper case to describe discourses that are generally accepted within a given community or organization:

> A Discourse is a socially accepted association among ways of using language, of thinking, feeling, believing, valuing, and of acting that can be used to identify oneself as a member of a socially meaningful group or social network or to signal (that one is playing) a socially meaningful role. (1990, p. 143)

Thus, the ways I dress, talk, act, interact, and even think positions me as a member of the teaching staff at my school. In fact, I have never been mistaken for a parent in my 15 years of teaching. Both official and unofficial expectations for teachers determine much about me and the types of social relationships in which I participate. However, as a member of the teaching staff, I also play particular roles and fulfill particular expectations within that discourse community. These roles position me within this discourse community and contribute to my individual identity as a teacher. As Gee reports, "Discourses are tied to particular social groups and the 'identities' their members take on when playing their apportioned 'roles' within the social practices of the group" (1992, p. 104).

Gee (1990) explains how discourses are socially constructed within the social histories of groups of people. Mainstream discourses are those discourses that support existing power structures and the institutions that sustain those power structures. These discourses contain "pervasive social theories" (p. 139) about the distribution of material goods and beliefs that the ways things are is both natural and inevitable. Fairclough (1989, 1993) emphasizes this ideological and political nature of discourses, focusing specifically on how discourses can mask implicit assumptions about our social world and differentially position groups of people.

At Rosa Parks Elementary School, where this research was completed, teachers were struggling to help children learn to read despite a difficult teaching situation. Our school had spent the past 3 years on the state list of low-performing schools and during the year in which this research project was conducted, we faced the possibility of being closed by the state if test scores in reading did not improve.

The voices of my colleagues convey the frustrations that often accompany teaching children in large urban schools, including working in large, impersonal, crowded, and sometimes hostile schools. Ashton (1986) reports that teachers in urban communities often lack faith in their own ability to motivate children and a sense of efficacy about themselves as teachers. Furthermore, larger schools, like those in urban areas, tend to be places where relationships between teachers and principals are often characterized by conflict. Principals in large schools tend to have poor attitudes about staff members, and teachers in large schools tend to be more authoritarian in their teaching styles. My colleagues were not bad people or bad teachers, but they were working under extreme pressure within a minimally supportive context. These frustrations contribute to teachers' willingness to blame parents. Twenty years ago, Sarah Lawrence-Lightfoot wrote:

> When teachers are not able to effectively communicate with minority children, when reading skills of children radically decline as they grow in years, when social control rather than education become the preoccupation of teachers, then schools displace the origins of failure onto families. (1978, p. 206)

As Grumet (1988) explains, educators' feelings about their own children do not extend to other people's children. The children of single parents, the urban poor, and people who do not resemble ourselves are described as "other," and myriad assumptions accompany the label. This labeling of poor people as "them" rather than "us" is deeply rooted and highly resistant to change (Apple, 1996). Urban parents are perceived by teachers in particular ways; as Winters notes, "In disadvantaged urban areas, [parents] are generally unrecognized, unappreciated, often dismissed, and considered by the public school system as having little to offer" (Winters, 1993, p. xvii).

Teachers often interpret parent behaviors as needy, naive, or hysterical and may perceive parents as working in opposition to their own efforts (Fine, 1993). Lawrence-Lightfoot explains that teachers often view parents as "threatening crowds" (1978, p. 201) rather than as individuals.

Beverly Gordon describes a "learned-discourse" acquired by teachers and teacher educators that refers to the "poor, jobless, the disenfranchised fringe dwellers of society, usually people of color" (1993, p. 224) as being the cause of their own difficulties; this perspective ignores the social and political dimensions of people's experiences that limit and define opportunity. Gordon argues for teachers to recognize the humanity of "the other" and encourages teachers to ask difficult questions about existing social situations that will lead them to interrogate these learned discourses.

I am certainly not immune to the effects of negative discourses. As described earlier, my first few weeks in the research field were full of surprises despite my having worked with families at Rosa Parks Elementary School for 8 years. Fortunately, during my years at Rosa Parks, I enjoyed close relationships with many of my students and their families. I regularly visited children's homes and got to know their parents and some of the struggles they face. While my colleagues often complained about parents not coming in for parent conferences, I had met with every parent twice a year for the past 3 years. These positive experiences caused me to begin to question many negative assumptions about urban parents that were so often voiced in the staff room and halls of my school. I had met some amazing parents and was beginning to suspect that apathy, disinterest, and neglect were not as common as urban educators and the society at large imagined. However, I too was surprised at the extent of parents' interest and involvement in reading as reflected in this research.

Despite my efforts to identify and name mainstream discourses, I am still not immune to their effects. Writing a book always involves risk. By putting words and thoughts on paper, writers always risk revealing their own biases and assumptions. I am suspect that there are places in the following pages where this occurs. My hope is that my foibles will provide opportunities for discussion and learning as we work together to become better teachers for all students.

THE PURPOSE OF THIS BOOK

This research is an attempt to systematically document the ways parents and children in one urban community conceptualize reading. These urban families are the focus of my research. As illustrated in the preceding pages, educators and the larger community often make assumptions about the families of my students. I suggest, however, that these assumptions are generally based on media depictions and an urban mythology that attempts to explain the academic difficulties of urban schools by blaming parents or offering simplistic notions of teacher incompetence (poor pedagogy, lazy and uncaring teachers). This research is an attempt to move beyond assumptions toward a richer understanding of the literate lives of my students and their families by revealing complexities that have previously been unknown and unrecognized.

In particular, I am interested in the ways urban students and their parents conceptualize the purposes of reading and how children learn to read. My methodology involves listening closely to the voices of students and parents to capture their voices and perspectives. What do parents perceive to be the difficulties their children face in becoming capable readers? What role do they view themselves as playing in helping their children learn to read? What are the challenges of learning to read in an urban school and community?

Insistence on listening to the voices of urban parents and community members is not a novel approach; many researchers have noted the importance of learning about urban communities from the residents themselves. Lawrence-Lightfoot suggests that part of the solution lies in parents and teachers building strong relationships: "Urban parents and teachers need to get to know each other in a more intuitive sense, which only arises out of hard work and experience coming together" (1978, p. 172).

More recently, Jill Sunday Bartoli has made a similar plea for urban teachers to move beyond assumptions, to get to know parents as individuals, as well as recognizing

> the students' potential, language ability, competence, maturity, and strengths. They [those who make assumptions] also did not look at the *real* family of the child behind the school and community assumptions and preconceptions, a view that could come only from an established relationship built on trust, meaningful communication, and genuine concern. (1995, p. 92)

Rather than blame parents, teachers can learn from them. As Lisa Delpit explains, teachers are in an ideal position to initiate "true dialogue" with parents.

This can only be done, however, by seeking out those [parents, students and community members] whose perspectives may differ most, by learning to give their words complete attention, by understanding one's own power, even if that power stems from being in the majority, by being unafraid to raise questions about discrimination and voicelessness with people of color, and to listen to, no, to *hear* what they say. I suggest that the results of such interactions may be the most powerful and empowering coalescence yet seen in the educational realm—for *all* teachers and for all the students they teach. (1995, p. 47)

Lawrence-Lightfoot (1978) describes how parents bring their children to school along with their own recollections of school. Lawrence-Lightfoot attributes African American parent noninvolvement to parents' inability to "negotiate the bureaucratic maze of schools or a response to a long history of exclusion and rejection at the school door" (p. 161). Bartoli (1995) describes how parents' school experiences often resulted in parents feeling estranged and disenfranchised from schools. Lawrence-Lightfoot (1978) explains that African American parents often view teachers as not believing that school can help their child; they believe that teachers do not push African American students because of the low expectations teachers have for their poor, urban students. These "hostile" (p. 167) stereotypes foster a sense of distance and distrust between teachers and students. Parents and teachers pull away from each other, and eventual school failure is blamed on the child and the family.

Too often, attempts to reach out to urban parents focus on the parents' perceived inadequacies. Parent-training classes that focus on both academic and nonacademic needs of parents are touted as solutions for poor, struggling, and minority families. Instead of listening to parents, recognizing the efforts parents make to support their children, and exploring the daily challenges that poor urban parents experience, parent training in poor urban communities generally involves "experts" telling parents what they should do.

It cannot be forgotten that urban children are learning to read within particular schools and community contexts. Inadequate funding, high teacher-to-student ratios, deteriorating facilities, high student and teacher mobility, substantial racial and socioeconomic differences between students and staff, and desperate attempts to raise student test scores contribute to the challenges my students face at school. The community offers additional concerns related to rampant poverty, a lack of community resources, unsafe neighborhoods, and socioeconomic and racial segregation. As parents of urban students attempt support their children as readers within these urban contexts, it is important to admit to ourselves that these are not the contexts in which we would choose to live or have our own children educated. There are good reasons for our reluctance to have our own children attend these schools and these reasons are equally poignant in the lives of my students and their families.

THE PLAN OF THIS BOOK

The pages that follow are filled with the voices of students and their parents. Their voices are too often dismissed, ignored, and discredited in educational forums. Each chapter of this book focuses on a particular theme that arose out of the research process.

Chapter One situates this research within a theoretical framework that emphasizes both sociocultural and sociopolitical aspects of learning to read in an urban school. Readers are introduced to mainstream discourses that circulate about urban families and the process of learning to read as well as the presence of alternative discourses that coexist alongside these mainstream discourses. In this chapter I also explore the limits of alternative discourses and the ways that mainstream discourses deny the possibility of alternative interpretations of reality. Finally, a section that defines and explores different types of capital is presented. In Chapter Two, I present a description of the methodology used in this research project.

In Chapter Three, I explore the role that reading plays in the lives of children and their parents. The chapter begins with parents' descriptions of reading that associate knowing how to read with "survival." These examples emphasize the critical role parents believe reading will play in their children's lives. Parent responses point to three ways that parents view reading as critical to "getting somewhere." These include reading for gaining viable employment, reading for physical mobility, and reading as an escape from daily life. The chapter concludes with data that explore how children and parents describe the repercussions of not being able to read.

Chapter Four opens with a discussion of the many ways parents report helping their children with reading. I then discuss "staying on" children, a concept that arose across many interviews. In this chapter, parents also describe teachers in their own lives who stayed on them when they were children and eventually shaped their expectations for their children's teachers. The chapter ends with students' comments that reflect their expectations of their teachers.

In Chapter Five, relationships between teachers, children, and parents are explored further. First, I examine the role parents believe they play in helping children learn to read and the parents' perceptions of who taught them how to read. Then, I explore the reading relationships that children share with teachers and their expectations of their teachers. Finally, I examine the social interactions that children share with their peers and siblings in relation to the act of reading.

Following a brief review of the theoretical work that defines the concept of reading identity, in Chapter Six I explore the ways that parents define themselves as competent readers yet distinguish themselves from "real" readers or "bookworms" and the social stigmas that accompany being a real reader. I then examine the ways parents' school experiences may have contributed to their hesitancy to define themselves as real readers.

In Chapter Seven, I examine many of the contradictions that exist between participants' invocation of mainstream discourses and the alternative discourses that they simultaneously present. This analysis leads to an awareness of the fragility and political vulnerability of alternative discourses and raises questions about the possibility that alternative discourses might lead to social change.

In Chapter Eight I present a case study of one family via a contextualized model of reading that is developed throughout this book. This family is also presented to allow us to explore the types and degrees of capital the family possesses; the case study further reinforces the idea that reading skills alone will not lead to social, economic, and political change for families. Finally, I make recommendations for teachers and educators interested in working toward the development of classrooms and schools that not only recognize and build upon the literacy experiences children bring to school but also demonstrate respect for alternative explanations for the difficulties children face when learning to read in urban schools.

1

A Theoretical Framework

Learning to read is both a social and a political process. Consider the following conversations I had with parents of two of my students:

> *Ms. Lilly*: Would your child be a better reader if he attended a suburban school?
>
> *Ms. Horner*: Mmm, that's hard, um, cause I've w—I think suburban schools are better than city schools.
>
> *Ms. Lilly*: And you've been in both.
>
> *Ms. Horner*: Yeah.
>
> *Ms. Lilly*: Why do you think suburban are better?
>
> *Ms. Horner*: I don't know. I think that they, they have more resources available to them. And um, I don't know. . . . When, when I went to school out in [neighboring suburban community] it was beautiful. Um, we had, there was so much around us to get into that was positive. You know. And um, I know that times have changed. I don't know what the suburban schools are like now, um, but I'm hoping that it is the same from um, when I went to school. I, I just think that there is, because they have so much available to them. Um, the doors are open more.
>
> *Ms. Lilly*: Do you think Christy would be a better reader, if she would have an easier time learning to read if she were in a suburban school?
>
> *Ms. Green*: Do you know, my answer's gonna be a bit weird I suppose. She might. They might have had better educational things. She might also have had a . . . harder time being mixed [biracial] in a suburban school. She might have had such a hard time that she couldn't learn. I don't know but I'm not going to live in a suburban area.

Both Ms. Horner's and Ms. Green's comments describe economic and social differences between urban and suburban schools. For both parents,

15

learning to read is not only contingent upon the teacher and the classroom, but also related to the school and the social context that exists within that school and community. These parents describe learning as situated within the child's social world and the political and economic realities of schools and the larger society.

As my students and their parents participated in a series of interviews, their words demonstrated the need for a theoretical framework that recognizes the importance of both social and political aspects of schooling. James Gee (1990) and others (Bakhtin, 1981, 1986; Voloshinov, 1973, 1983; Wertsch, 1990) are concerned with how language and thought are situated within cultural, historical, and institutional settings. Specifically, sociocultural approaches to education situate learning within a dynamic that recognizes language as a social construction that operates within schools and the larger society. Through social interaction and participation in particular discourse communities, children acquire social norms and fulfill social expectations (Gee, 1990). A sociocultural approach helps us to understand the process of learning to read within the context of students' lives and their social worlds.

Sociopolitical approaches to education (Apple, 1979, 1996; Apple & Christian-Smith, 1991; Giroux, 1992; Giroux & McLaren 1994; Luke, 1995a, 1995b; McLaren, 1988, 1989; New London Group, 1996) reveal the ways social, economic, and political forces reward and punish people according to social variables, including race, class, and gender. Sociopolitical approaches also remind us that certain social groups dominate resources while other groups tend to be subjugated in accordance with differences (Apple, 1979, 1996; Giroux, 1992; Luke, 1995a).

However, sociocultural and sociopolitical theories are not separate, distinct theories. In many instances the sociocultural and sociopolitical approaches overlap and converge by virtue of their adherents recognizing the ways social, economic, and political contexts affect the lives and experiences of individuals within particular communities. However, mainstream discourses about learning to read often deny the existence of both sociocultural and sociopolitical contexts in the process of learning to read. Learning to read is often condensed to the acquisition of discrete skills and item knowledge that are assumed to spontaneously manifest themselves into a reading process. In this book I challenge these mainstream assumptions about reading by revealing how learning to read and the act of reading are social and political acts that occur within urban schools, communities, and families.

In this chapter, I will present a theoretical framework that will be used to make sense of the reading experiences and beliefs of my students and their families. I will first explore mainstream discourses about reading and about urban families. I will then explore the ways these discourses operate in educational forums and the possibilities presented by alternative discourses that challenge these mainstream discourses. Intersections of race and class within urban schools will be considered, followed by a discussion of cultural capital and the manner in which it operates in the lives of my students.

MAINSTREAM DISCOURSES ABOUT READING

> When her family moved to a new city, Kathy Dunford realized her daughter Courtney, then 6, could read but did not know the rules to sound out a word. Working with tutor Kelly Ricards helped Courtney become a capable reader. "Now she's a real eager learner," says her mom. (Seal, 2000)

Thus begins an article written for parents that appeared in *Family Circle,* a mainstream "women's" magazine. What interests me is the emphasis placed on the importance of "sounding out words" despite the mother's assertion that her child could read. Knowing the rules for sounding out words is presented as essential within the mainstream discourses that surround the process of learning to read in the United States. While many reading experts (Adams, 1990; Chall, Jacobs, & Baldwin, 1990; Clay, 1991; Goodman, 1996; Weaver, 1994) maintain that sounding out words constitutes only a very small part of the reading process, mainstream accounts of reading continue to emphasize its importance.

Mainstream discourses about reading are also evident in the commodification of reading in North American society. Patrick Shannon (2001) explores the popularity of "phonics toys" and programs on audiotape designed to teach children reading skills. The marketability of these reading products is contingent on people believing that they will help children learn to read. The types of reading practices that proliferate in American homes and schools also reveal mainstream discourses about reading and learning to read:

- teaching children the names of each letter;
- teaching children to be able to recognize words in any context;
- discouraging children from relying on illustrations to read;
- having children copy words to help them learn to read; and
- having children learn new words by practicing with flashcards.

While several of these beliefs and practices would be challenged by reading experts (Adams, 1990; Chall et al., 1990; Clay, 1991; Goodman, 1996;

Weaver, 1994), the practices continue to flourish in homes and classrooms across the country because they are generally associated with learning to read. As Trevor Cairney reports, "Teachers, students and parents construct particular models and definitions of literacy and sanction particular understandings, norms, expectations, and roles that define what it means to be literate" (Cairney & Ruge, 1997, p. 6). Allan Luke and Peter Freebody (1997) report that reading is historically understood to be a set of neutral skills rather than a "social epistemology" that is defined through social contexts in which it is learned and used. These conceptions of reading are created and supported by people's own school experiences, media depictions of classrooms, and the commercialization of products designed to help children learn discrete skills associated with reading (Shannon, 2001).

Finally, mainstream discourses about reading present reading as a salve for the social and economic inequities of modern society. Consider this quote from *Children's Literature and Critical Theory*, a children's literature text:

> Reading is essential in America, even if it means only reading labels on food containers, logos of companies, or street and highway signs. This rudimentary decoding allows us to control our day-to-day activities and decisions. If we cannot read the label on a can in the grocery market, we cannot understand how many additives or preservatives have been used and we cannot determine which product is best for us. When we cannot follow a road map, we are afraid that we will get lost in a strange city and are less apt to travel. Not understanding written job memos means loss of power. Reading is a basic skill for living in today's modern world. (May, 1995, p. 38)

Learning to read is presented as critical for success and survival. Although Harvey Graff's (1979) historical study of illiterate people in the 19th century strongly challenged this assumption, in the 20 years since his work was published, the assumed causal bond between literacy and both economic and social success has remained entrenched in the American psyche.

MAINSTREAM DISCOURSES ABOUT URBAN FAMILIES

As described in the introduction, mainstream discourses about urban families infect my thoughts and the thoughts of my colleagues. Urban teachers are susceptible to dominant discourses that permeate schools and society and characterize our students' families as ineffective, uninterested in education, pathological, and illiterate. Figure 1.1 presents a sample parent contract that parents might be asked to sign so that their third- and fourth- grade children could participate in an extended-day program designed to improve student achievement on state tests. Asking parents to make a written commitment to supporting their children reveals assumptions that have been made by school district officials. Apparently, district officials have assumed that many urban parents do not support their children or monitor their children's progress and attendance. Officials have also assumed that the child's home may not be "conducive to learning" and that parental communication with staff may not be "positive." This brief 50-word document reveals that a range of assumptions have been made about my students and their families. Thus assumptions about urban families are not unique to teachers; administrators and policy makers are also susceptible.

Yet discourses incorporate more than written messages; the acts that accompany this parent contract also contribute to the construction of

Figure 1.1. Parent Contract.

After-School Academy
Parent Contract

I, the parent/guardian of _____, agree to the following terms as part of the After School Academy.

I will:

- support my child and the program staff.

- provide an environment in the home which is conducive to learning.

- monitor my child's progress and attendance in the ASA.

- be responsible for my child's safe transportation from the tutoring site.

- communicate with the program staff in an ongoing, positive manner.

_____   _____

(Parent's/Guardian's Signature)   (Date)

_____

(Phone Number)

---

negative discourses about urban families. The idea that parents are asked to sign a written contract speaks loudly about our expectations for urban parents. As a suburban, middle-class parent, I am not asked to sign documents attesting that my home is conducive to learning or that I will "support my child and the program staff." The suburban district that my daughter attends trusts me to do these things. However, the trust that I enjoy as a suburban, middle-class parent is not extended to the parents of my students. The interviews recorded in the chapters that follow illustrate the words of James Gee:

> [Mainstream] Discourses often conflict seriously (in values, attitudes, ways of thinking or talking) with their own home and community-based discourses. Furthermore, these mainstream Discourses often incorporate attitudes and values hostile to, and even in part define themselves in opposition to, these minority students and their home and community-based Discourses. (1990, p. 148)

Thus, as my students are learning the letters of the alphabet, grasping basic concepts about the way English print functions, and reading engaging and interesting texts, they are also exposed to subtle and insidious discourses about their families and themselves that position them and their families in ways that deny and dismiss nonmainstream ways of thinking, talking, and knowing.

DISCOURSES IN EDUCATION

Earlier in this book, I used the words of James Gee to present discourses as "anagrams of particular ways of talking, viewing, thinking, believing, interacting, acting, and sometimes reading and writing" (1992, p. 104). Successful use of a particular discourse indicates membership in a particular social group. For example, there are ways of talking, viewing, thinking, and so on that would distance me from the other teachers at school and might even cost me my teaching job. Mainstream discourses about how teachers talk, think, interact, and act define the acceptable parameters of teaching.

While mainstream discourses that describe reading as a neutral and skills-based process deny the sociocultural and sociopolitical aspects of teaching and learning, mainstream discourses about urban families position and portray urban parents in ways that deny and devalue their interest in their children as readers. These mainstream discourses serve an important role in society. By blaming parents for the reading difficulties of children, these discourses absolve teachers, schools, and the larger society of responsibility for the educational challenges of urban students. They maintain the existence of a underpaid, undereducated workforce and contribute to the continuation of racism and classism in our society. By blaming victims for their own difficulties, these discourses provide a rationale for the existence of poverty, substandard living conditions, and hunger. Allan Luke explains, "Discourse has a hegemonic function. Its principal effect is to establish itself as a form of common sense, to naturalize its own functions through its appearance in everyday texts" (1995b, p. 20).

Fairclough (1989) maintains that established social and political organizations have a vested interest in maintaining as common sense those ideological assumptions that benefit established social and political institutions. These mainstream discourses support the continuation of established, powerful organizations as they constantly work to maintain their dominance. Schools contribute to the dominance of mainstream ways of thinking; Lynn Fendler writes that

> to be subjected to education has meant to be disciplined according to a regimen of remembering and forgetting, of assuming identities normalized through discursive practices, and of a history of unpredictable diversions. (1998, p. 61)

Susan Hill et al. (1998) explain that the social environment is neither "neutral or benign"; it is "often directive, controlling and heavily invested in the individual's acquiring some ideas and avoiding others (p. 36)."

Fairclough (1989) writes of the "opacity of discourse" (p. 41) and explains that people are often unaware of the political and social ideologies implicit within particular discourses. According to Fairclough, the "opacity of discourse" operates in three ways. First, discourses become opaque when the meanings of words and situations become naturalized and remain unquestioned. In my research, teachers, including myself, along with the larger public, too often accept stereotypes about urban families; too often educators assume that urban families do not value reading, without taking the time to talk with parents, learn about their lives, and discover their true feelings. Mainstream discourses that bring with them assumptions about urban families are rarely recognized, much less challenged, by people who occupy positions of authority within established social institutions. This is because these mainstream discourses tend to reflect and confirm the social understandings of the people who populate these mainstream institutions. In this book, mainstream ways of thinking, which often remain opaque and unrecognized, will be questioned and challenged through the words of my students and their families.

Second, discourses become opaque through the naturalization of interactive routines. In schools, these are the unquestioned routine classroom and school practices that include the teacher giving directions, students raising their hands, and students responding appropriately. They also include parents being contacted about student misbehavior, parents being invited to the school for conferences, and teachers being expected to provide parents with advice on helping their children to learn at home. These routines are assumed to lead to student learning and have become the repertoire that parents and teachers rely on to guide their interactions with each other. Through engaging parents in ongoing interviews, this research project disrupted these naturalized routines, providing the opportunity for both parents and the teacher-researcher to operate outside expected norms, by facilitating the discussion of issues that went beyond those generally discussed at teacher conferences and by creating personal relationships that generally do not develop between teachers and parents.

Finally, discourses also become opaque through the naturalization of subject positions. In schools, teachers are assumed to be the experts on learning to read. Parents are expected to support the teacher's agenda and rely on the teacher for advice on helping their child to succeed in school. In my school, this subject positioning is complicated by race and class differences that often separate teachers and parents and exaggerate the social distance between players, creating a fertile space for the construction of negative assumptions about the other.

Alternative Discourses

While mainstream discourses often remain unchallenged within mainstream contexts, the dominance of mainstream discourses is constantly being challenged by alternative ways of viewing the world. Alternative discourses are ways of understanding and describing the world that are grounded in people's lived experiences. These alternative conceptions of reality are not less accurate or less informed than mainstream discourses. Alternative discourses are not merely interesting phenomena or instances of exotic cultural practices. Alternative discourses represent people's lived realities and their essential understandings about their world.

In the chapters that follow, the parents of the children I teach challenge the same mainstream discourses that they cite. When mainstream discourses fail to account for the difficulties children face with learning to read, alternative discourses, grounded in people's lived experiences, are used by the parents to explain the role of reading in their lives and the reasons for the difficulties experienced by their children and their children's peers. Mainstream and alternative discourses about the world are constantly in contention and are never static (Fairclough, 1989); mainstream discourses and alternative discourses are constantly evolving and redefining themselves partly through the ongoing struggle between these conflicting ways of viewing the world.

Parents challenge the existence of a direct relationship between reading and gaining viable employment. Through their own examples, they challenge mainstream notions of urban parents as uninterested, illiterate, and uninformed. Parents suggest reasons beyond a lack of parenting skills and intelligence to explain the difficulties their children may experience in learning to read.

Jerome Bruner explains that scientific psychology

> will achieve a more effective stance toward the culture at large when it comes to recognize that the folk psychology of ordinary people is not *just* a set of self-assuaging illusions but the culture's beliefs and working hypothesis about what makes it possible and fulfilling for people to live together even with great personal sacrifice. (1986, p. 32)

In the chapters that follow, I explore the alternative discourses used by parents and children and how these discourses contribute to my students' and their parents' understandings about reading.

The data I have collected remind us that mainstream discourses and alternative discourses are not mutually exclusive. Mainstream and alternative discourses often coexist within cultural groups and within individual psyches. For example, when asked about the reasons why parents at my school do not attend parent conferences, Ms. Webster replied:

> I don't know. With me, I can't be there because of me working but there's a lot of parents that don't work; they [are] just lazy. They just don't want to go in. . . . They don't want to waste their time because they gonna hear the same old same old. That's what they feel.

Ms. Webster adopts the mainstream discourse about lazy, uninterested, urban parents to explain the behavior of "a lot of parents." However, she offers an alternative discourse relating to work obligations to explain her own difficulties in attending parent conferences. Finally, she offers an additional alternative discourse that criticizes teachers for failing to make parent conferences worthwhile and productive experiences. Mainstream and alternative discourses are both evoked in this brief text.

Jennifer Gore describes "different discursive strands that operate alongside one another" (1993, p. 56). Bruner (1986) explains that a person may utilize both mainstream discourse and his or her own theories about the world and yet remain consciously unaware of the ideological contradiction between the two.

Based on their interviews with poor and working-class African American men, Fine and Weis (1998) argue that these men explain their situations in contradictory ways. While they voice an extensive critique of society that points to racism and limited opportunities, they simultaneously attribute their own difficulties to personal failure. While these explanations are contradictory, as Fine and Weis note, their emphasis on personal accomplishment reaffirms their confidence in African American youth by supporting the notion that success is possible for themselves and their peers given the proper effort and attitude.

However, Fairclough (1989) suggests that it is within these contradictions that new possibilities arise; he believes that commonsense assumptions are "fore-grounded" (p. 106) when things go wrong in people's lives, when there is a large enough gap between the perspectives of two speakers, or when there is a deliberate disturbance of the commonsense mainstream discourse. Fairclough (1989, 1993, 1995) advocates a critical approach to the analysis of discourse that reveals how commonsense assumptions implicit in discourses are shaped by power and ideology. This process enables people to view situations and experiences as ideologically laden and enables people to act in ways that challenge mainstream interpretations. As I share the words of my students and their parents, my goal is to disrupt existing mainstream discourses that position urban parents in particular ways and present alternate interpretations of the difficulties urban students face as they learn to read. Furthermore, in this book I will explore the contradictions that exist between mainstream and alternative accounts of reading and learning to read in an urban community.

The Limits of Alternative Discourses

Ms. Holt was not only the mother of Bradford and another son who was 3 years older than Bradford, but also of five older children who were in high school and beyond at the time of the interviews. I asked Ms. Holt what changed as her children grew older.

> I have no [idea], if I knew I would . . . put it in a pill form and give it to . . . a middle school and high school. Whatever it was [that kids need] and they [her own kids] had that, whatever drive they had in grammar school, if you could bottle it. Cause I don't know what happens—usually in middle school, between grammar school and middle school and high school it just, it seems to just

lose interest. I don't know what it is whether it's peer pressure or what it is. They just don't have to, I don't know, I, I have no idea. I, I do, I really wish I knew because there are so many, we're losing so many of our young kids.

In this quote, Ms. Holt tries to explain the changes that occurred for her children as they grew older. However, her difficulties in explaining this phenomena are apparent not only in her inability to find the right words but also in her faltering speech. She cites one mainstream discourse about peer pressure but remains unconvinced; other mainstream discourses often invoked to explain the difficulties of urban students include a lack of parental involvement, laziness, and intellectual inferiority. However, Ms. Holt does not offer those possibilities. Throughout the interviews, there were many times when words proved elusive as participants tried to convey their thoughts. This happened when parents refused to accept mainstream discourses; explanations that offered the potentiality of alternative discourses often defied expression.

Thus, the possibility of alternative discourses contributing to social change is limited not only by dominant discourses but also by the difficulties people face when attempting to name alternative ways of knowing the world. This tendency for speakers to resort to "I don't know" as they struggle to present alternative explanations for their world will be explored further in Chapter Seven. While the existence of alternative discourses presents the possibility of alternative ideological interpretations of the world and challenges to mainstream interpretations of reality, alternative discourses are generally silenced and refuted via the dominance of mainstream discourses.

Furthermore, institutionalized practices such as receiving welfare payments and free school lunches stigmatize individuals, creating a situation in which individuals have difficulty being heard as a result of this stigma. Ms. Johnson, one of my students' parents, describes her experiences:

I think when you go to different stores and things people look at you, especially when you have the food stamps. Or even when you go to the medical doctors or whatever and you whip out the Medicaid card and they give you a weird look. I've been through all of that and I'm glad I work.

Erving Goffman explains how stigmatizing factors affect individuals:

By definition, of course, we believe that a person with a stigma is not quite human. On this assumption we exercise varieties of discrimination, through which we effectively, if often unthinkingly, reduce his life chances. We construct a stigma-theory and ideology to explain his inferiority and account for the danger he represents, sometimes rationalizing an animosity based on other differences, such as those of social class. (Lemert & Branaman, 1997, p. 73)

Stigma contributes to the tendency for alternative discourses to be denied and dismissed. When individual speakers are perceived as inferior, their voices are silenced within the din of naturalized mainstream discourses.

In the case of urban parents and students, alternative discourses explain the academic difficulties of urban children as being caused by complex interactions of culture, race, politics, and economics rather than simply poor parenting; they report positive contributions that urban parents make to support their children as they learn to read; and they lead to an examination of the challenges that define life for urban families rather than blaming urban families for their own difficulties. However, the effects of alternative discourses are severely limited by the dominance of mainstream discourses, the elusiveness of words that adequately express alternative discourses, and the stigmatization and social positioning of speakers.

Discourses, Reading, Race, and Class

During a recent walk through the mall, my 7-year-old daughter asked me an important question: "Mom, why are the children at your school mostly Black and the kids at my school mostly White?" I was tempted to give her the easy answer and explain that it was just because the children who live in the neighborhoods near my school happen to be African American, but that answer denies the historical and current relationships that exist between race, class, and opportunity. Instead, I drew a long breath and explained that many of the families at my school had suffered and continue to suffer social inequities related to their race and class. I tried to describe a few of the factors that contribute to the struggles faced by the families of my students, including racial discrimination, inadequate educational opportunities, and the lack of viable employment opportunities. At seven years old my daughter is already beginning to identify social inequities in our world; I am certain that my students are aware of them as well.

In listening to the voices of my students and their parents, I do not want to ignore the roles that race and racism play in our lives. As amalgamations of particular ways of talking, thinking, valuing, interacting, acting, and reading and writing (Gee, 1992) discourses are constituted through group participation that often align with race, class, or both. It is important to recognize that differences between discourses can become criteria for including or excluding people. Thus, while most school districts would deny any racist intent behind policies, students are routinely judged by how they talk, interact, and write. A student who writes a thoughtful and content-rich paper but also accesses linguistic resources from his or her home discourses runs the risk of poor evaluation. While I agree with Lisa Delpit (1995) that all students need and deserve the opportunity to master mainstream discourses to enable them to fully participate in mainstream society, sensitivity to three issues is necessary. These three issues reveal the mechanisms through which many schools are complacent in the systematic oppression and dismissal of children whose home discourses differ from those of the mainstream.

First, it must be remembered that there are children, among them my daughter, who have a great advantage because their home discourse, or primary discourse, aligns with the discourses they confront when they enter school. The ways they act, interact, value, and even think are consonant with the discourse practices they encounter in the classroom. In contrast, my African American and Hispanic students must often acquire the dominant discourse; the discourses that my students learn at home are their primary discourses. The discourse they learn in school is a secondary discourse. As Gee reminds us:

> Mainstream middle-class children often acquire school-based literacies through experiences in the home both before and during school, as well as by the opportunities school gives them to practice what they are acquiring. Children from non-mainstream homes often do not get the opportunities to acquire dominant secondary Discourses (for example, those connected to school) prior to school in their homes due to the lack of access their parents have to these secondary Discourses. When coming to school, they cannot practice what they haven't got, and they are exposed to mostly a process of learning and not acquisition. (1990, p. 156)

While my students are unquestionably capable of mastering mainstream ways of talking, thinking, valuing, interacting, acting, reading, and writing, they have a much more complicated trajectory to negotiate. The advantages that my daughter brings to school, resulting only from the circumstances of her birth, privilege her in the classroom. Because of the advantages that she and other children enjoy, comparisons of children, especially those as young as age 9, on standardized reading and writing tests are particularly insidious and are better indicators of children's access to mainstream discourse than they are measures of children's learning.

Thus evaluation systems that measure student mastery of discourse conventions inherently favor and penalize students along lines that roughly correspond to race and class.

Second, it must also be remembered that the alternative discourses that children bring to school reflect useful, powerful, and productive ways of being and making sense of the world. Although acquisition of mainstream discourses may benefit my students in some, perhaps many, contexts, alternative discourses challenge mainstream interpretations and understandings; these contradictions present the possibility of change and a challenge to the dominance of mainstream discourses. If children are expected to adopt mainstream discourses in school to the exclusion of their home discourses, alternative ways of understanding the world are silenced in schools and the continued dominance of mainstream discourses is assured. When African American and Hispanic children are silenced, covert forms of racism are in operation.

Finally, we must not forget that discourses are often used as "gates" to ensure that only the right people get access to particular opportunities and institutions (Gee, 1990). Because discourses are social constructions shared within groups of people, people in particular groups can be denied access to resources based on their lack of mastery of dominant discourses. Again, intersections among race, class, and discourses make access to these resources more difficult for some children.

THE POSSESSION OF CAPITAL

Ms. Rodriguez offers a story about Alisa's younger sister, Quanza, who is in kindergarten.

> Quanza has lost [her] gloves and I had just bought her a pair of gloves. And I find out [imitating Quanza] "I lost them." And I said, "When I get paid I'll buy you another pair," right? Her teacher assumed I was on welfare. . . . [She] said, "Tell your mother when she get her check to buy you another pair of gloves." And I went to school and told her, "Let me explain something to you, OK? I work, everyday. Don't tell my child to tell me that, OK? When I get some money I'll go buy her a pair of gloves. I don't need you or nobody else to tell me that. I know her hands are cold. That's why most of the time she wear my gloves [on the way to school] but I take them from her when I got to go to work, thank you . . . because most of the time when they leave from school my girl-

friend['s] husband is down there and he drive them home. I don't get no ride home. I walk." So she looked at me like excuse me, I'm sorry. [I told her] "That's OK, be careful."

Quanza's teacher has made some assumptions about Quanza and her family; she has assumed not only that Ms. Rodriguez is on welfare, but also that she does not realize that her 5-year-old daughter needs gloves. Notably, Ms. Rodriguez brings to the teacher's attention the precautions she has taken to ensure that Quanza will not suffer without gloves (sharing her own gloves, arranging rides home). Ms. Rodriguez's resourcefulness has gone unrecognized by Quanza's teacher. In several ways, this story told by Ms. Rodriguez reveals her family's lack of institutionally recognized "cultural capital."

Pierre Bourdieu (1986) devised the term *capital* to describe cultural advantages that groups of people possess that favor them within a particular social context. These advantages relate to a variety of traits, including ethnicity, language, appearance, wealth, access to resources, education, and deportment. Differences in the amounts and types of capital people possess affect their social positioning and thus affect the ways people are positioned within a particular social context. Just prior to telling this story, Ms. Rodriguez spoke about the assumptions that teachers make about urban families: "A lot of teachers in a lot of schools they figure you live in a low, and, they say this is the ghetto, right? And they say a lot of people is in the ghetto so they assume everybody is on welfare." Ms. Rodriguez clearly understands that being poor and living in this particular community positions her in particular ways that not only permit teachers to make assumptions about her but also allow teachers to tell her child what she should be doing as a parent.

Bourdieu (1986) recognizes three forms of capital that people can possess: economic capital, cultural capital, and social capital. Cultural capital can take three forms: embodied capital, objectified capital, and institutional capital. *Embodied capital* refers to the mannerisms and social practices exhibited by a particular type of person. Saying the right things, dressing in an appropriate way, and using a particular set of manners constitute the possession of embodied capital. Embodied capital would also include fulfilling particular expectations around child rearing that include the expectation that parents provide children with gloves on cold days. While Ms. Rodriguez's resourcefulness is evident in her attempts to keep Quanza's fingers warm without gloves (i.e., sharing her own gloves, arranging rides), these skills and abilities go unrecognized by Quanza's teachers. The hegemony of assumptions that accompany living in the "ghetto" obfuscate the skills and abilities Ms. Rodriguez brings to parenting. Her response to the problem is unrecognized and dismissed.

Objectified capital includes documents or other artifacts that are recognized as having value within a particular community. In this situation, the teacher has identified gloves as being valuable; however, Ms. Rodriguez does not possess the economic resources to be able to attain these gloves immediately. Objectified capital is almost always contingent on the possession of economic capital.

Finally, *institutional capital* includes academic credentials and certificates that demonstrate particular accomplishments. Ms. Rodriguez's work toward the completion of her day-care certification is also unrecognized when the teacher assumes that she does not know or care enough to keep her child's hands warm.

In addition to cultural capital, people also control economic capital and social capital. *Economic capital* refers to money (Bourdieu, 1986). Ms. Rodriguez's lack of immediately available economic capital is the cause of Quanza being without gloves. Finally, *social capital* refers to a person's ability to gain access to cultural institutions and organizations; this access may be partially determined by a person's race, class and gender. Interestingly, Ms. Rodriguez makes the decision to approach the teacher and confront the teacher's assumptions about the situation. Whether this confrontation with the teacher resulted in any changes on the part of the individual teacher is unknown; however, the institutionally ingrained proclivity for teachers at my school to make assumptions about the families of our students certainly remains unshaken by one mother's conversation with her child's teacher.

As Bourdieu (1986) states, in order for the possession of any form of capital to advantage a person, capital must be institutionally legitimated and acknowledged by people with power; that is, "capital is only capital if it is recognized as such; this is if it is granted legitimacy, symbolic capital, with a larger social and cultural field" (Luke, 1996, p. 329). This is exactly the situation Ms. Rodriguez found herself in. Amid the deafening roar of mainstream discourses about poor, urban, single-parent families, the strengths and abilities Ms. Rodriguez brought to the classroom door remained unrecognized and thus unlegitimated. The person in authority, the teacher, failed to recognize and respect the abilities and resourcefulness that Ms. Rodriguez brought to a difficult situation. Having to share her own gloves and arranging rides for her child my not have been in the teachers' realm of experiences and thus were not considered as possibilities. This lack of capital also contributes to the difficulty in allowing alternative discourses to be heard within mainstream society.

CONCLUSION

The issues and ideas presented in this chapter are not just theoretical constructs that combine to present a theoretical framework for this book. These constructs are windows that reveal the ways in which power operates in my school and school community. When the words of my students and their families are presented alongside these theoretical positions, we can begin to dismiss and challenge simplistic explanations for the difficulties my students confront as they learn to read. My students, their families, and their teachers, including myself, are positioned in ways that vastly complicate the process of learning to read. While mainstream discourses narrowly describe reading as involving the acquisition of specific reading skills, the words of parents, teachers, administrators, and community members reveal the sociocultural and sociopolitical interests that surround my students and their families in their quest for reading. Furthermore, the minimal degrees of capital accessible to the families of my students positions them and the alternative discourses they offer at the margins of public discussions about literacy learning in urban schools.

This chapter has certainly not exhausted the range of issues and considerations that accompany learning to read in a poor urban community. In the chapters that follow, additional dimensions of learning to read will be explored.

2

Research Methodology

Viewing reading as situated within the social, economic, and political contexts of the community in which I teach requires a research methodology that captures my students' and their parents' personal experiences related to reading and learning to read as well as the issues, attitudes, and experiences that surround reading within this community. This research takes its place alongside a growing number of studies in which research is conducted and interpreted within local sites with the aim of beginning to identify the ways learning is situated within particular communities. Marie Clay explains, "We can escape the straitjacket of socioeconomic classifications of parents in our research and explore the reading practices, activities, systems and processes occurring in different families" (1996, p. x) in order to develop a clearer understanding of what reading means in particular communities.

As I designed this research study, I intended to accomplish two goals. First, I intended to situate discussions about reading within my students' personal and collective experiences. Through an acknowledgment of the existence of contextual factors that affect children as they learn to read, this research will foreground the ways contextual factors define the process of learning to read.

Second, I aimed to present the beginnings of a theoretical model that would explain how children's concepts about reading are situated within larger contexts that include a variety of situational and cultural factors. These include reading practices at home and in school; social, economic, and political contexts that define people's experiences with reading; various discourses that circulate concerning reading; and people's personal life experiences with reading.

To accomplish these goals, I have applied qualitative research methods that have proved successful for other researchers working with urban children and their families. Interviews, transcripts of classroom discussions, field notes, and samples of children's work are all types of data that other researchers have used to reveal the ways school, and more specifically reading, is situated within the lives and experiences of people (Bartoli, 1995; Dyson, 1993, 1997; Heath, 1983; Nieto, 1996; Purcell-Gates, 1995; Taylor, 1991, 1996; Taylor & Dorsey-Gaines, 1988). Carolyn Frank advocates that teachers apply enthographic techniques similar to those used by researchers, to "observe classrooms more efficiently, without making quick, critical evaluations or 'leaps to judgment'" (1999, p. 1).

SITE AND PARTICIPANTS

Rosa Parks Elementary School is a large urban elementary school (more than 850 students) that serves the poorest neighborhood of a midsized, northeastern city. Ninety-seven percent of the children at Rosa Parks qualify for free or reduced lunches. Between 94% and 98% of students qualify for Title I services. Rosa Parks has a very high mobility rate with as much as a third of classes changing between September and June.

At the time of this study, Rosa Parks was the only upstate elementary school to be on the State Education Department list of "Schools In Performance Review." If evidence of improvement on state reading tests at Grade 4 was not evident during the spring in which this research was conducted, our school would lose its charter and be disbanded. Over the past 10 years, numerous changes had been made at the school to try and address problems with reading instruction. A new principal was appointed, the open-classroom structure of the school was abandoned and walls were erected between classrooms, and a variety of instructional programs came and went, including Open Court, Distar, and two literature-centered basal reading series. Recently, the Reading Recovery Program was implemented to support struggling first-grade students and a local consultant was hired to improve reading instruction at Rosa Parks Elementary School.

During a visit to our school, State Education Department representatives noted that children were engaged in learning and that the school facility was clean and attractively decorated with student work. However, representatives noted a lack of continuity within the reading program, with children in different classrooms offered educational experiences that did not align within or across grade levels. In addition, state representatives observed a preponderance of teacher-directed instruction and voiced their belief that the school lacked a unified philosophy on how to implement a developmentally appropriate early childhood program. Perhaps most revealing was their contention that teachers subscribed to a deficit view of children characterized by low expectations for both student behavior and academic achievement. Despite these criticisms of our school and the local media's attempts to sensationalize our struggles, the parents I interviewed maintained faith in the school and its teachers. As Mr. Sherwood explained, "The school down here [pointing down the street toward where the school is located] is a good school and I think they can, ya'll can turn it around." Other parents referred to their own children's experiences; Ms. Hernandez reports, "I think they are doing great because Jasmine shocked me when she started learning how to read. I think you [the school staff] are doing a great job in reading."

At Rosa Parks Elementary School, classes were formed using a standard set of criteria (heterogeneous groupings based on student achievement, gender, and behavior). On the basis of school practices and policies, my class differed in no way from other first-grade classes in the building. Over the course of the research year, 31 children were moved in or out of my class. Although my class size averaged approximately 23 students, 31 different children were placed in my classroom over the course of the school year because of the school's high mobility rate. Permission was granted by parents of all children in the class—with the exception of one student who was only in our class for 3 months—to participate in the research project.

Children at Rosa Parks generally entered first grade at 5 to 7 years of age. In my class, three children were repeating Grade 1. Two others were a year older than their classmates, having started kindergarten a year later or attending a prefirst program. Most of the students were African American. Some had family ties to the Caribbean, while other students spoke of extended family members from "down South." The class included three Hispanic children with families from Puerto Rico and three multiracial children. While all children could be characterized as urban, poor, and from minority populations, their family backgrounds were quite diverse. All students were English dominant.

The parents of children in my class represented an equally broad range of individuals. Among the parents I interviewed, some were unemployed, while others had steady jobs. Some parents were on welfare; others had not been on welfare since they were children. One parent had earned an associate degree; other parents had not graduated from high school. Parents of children in my class grew up in cities, were raised down South, lived in suburban communities, and were raised in small rural towns. Some were single parents, others were married or had long-term relationships. One parent was Puerto Rican, three were European American, and six were African American. Most parents I spoke with had gone back to school after high school and were working to make a better life for their children.

While all children in the class participated in classroom activities that were part of the research project, 10 parent-child focus teams were randomly selected to participate in a series of interviews. With one exception, the selection process entailed my telephoning parents in alphabetical order from my class list. One parent who did not have a phone was contacted personally.

Ten focus families were established at the onset of the project. One mother chose not to continue beyond the first interview although she allowed me to continue interviews with her daughter. No reason was offered. Another parent and her child moved outside the school area in March but at the mother's request, they continued to participate in the project.

Focus parents who participated in this study were thanked with small gifts I provided on each of my visits; these included such things as jars of candy, pen and pencil sets, and gift sets of bath products. On my final visit, I brought each family a gift card for 20 dollars in merchandise at a local grocery store; children were brought books or were taken out for lunch or ice cream at a local restaurant.

DATA COLLECTION

Data collected included focus student and parent interviews, examples of student writing, student portfolios, daily field notes, lesson plans, and student reading levels as determined by the "text level" portion of the "Observation Survey" (Clay, 1993). In this section, I will briefly describe the data collected and its contribution to this research.

Parent Interviews

Focus parents participated in a series of four interviews aimed at identifying parent concepts about reading, parent experiences with reading, parental hopes and fears for their child as a reader, parent perceptions of appropriate school reading methods, and parent perceptions of what may hinder their child in learning to read. These interviews occurred between December 1996 and August 1997, approximately every other month, and generally in participants' homes.

Although I wrote a series of interview questions for each of the four formal interviews, these questions served as a guide rather than a strict outline; questions were asked in a sequence that seemed comfortable conversationally. Typically some questions led to interesting comments, while others seemed confusing to participants or appeared to hinder conversation; these latter questions were omitted from or revised for future interviews.

My questions often led parents to raise related issues, and parents often spoke at length about issues that concerned them without prompts from the researcher. Parents often used narratives or character descriptions of significant people in their lives to explain their understandings about reading. These stories helped me as the researcher to understand the connections that participants were making between their own childhood experiences at home and in school, their current lives, and the educational experiences of their children.

Later interviews often included questions related to comments that parents or students had made in earlier interviews. Sharing this information with parents gave me the opportunity to explore the generalizability of comments made by a particular parent and to test themes as they evolved from the data.

Student Interviews

Like their parents, students participated in a series of four interviews. Initial and final student interviews were adapted from the "Emergent Reader and Writer Interview" developed by a group of teachers from Denver, Colorado (Rhodes & Shanklin, 1993). In the final interview, I repeated questions asked in the initial interview, hoping that this might reveal interesting changes as my first-grade students learned to read; this was not the case. In the remaining two interviews, students were asked a variety of questions based on their responses to initial questions as well as questions evolving out of prior interviews and themes discussed in parent interviews. Students were questioned about their feelings about reading, what they thought good readers do, who needs to be able to read, and how children learn to read.

In general, student responses were less detailed than those of their parents. Students tended to answer questions directly and rarely used narrative to express themselves. When prompted to elaborate on a particular response, students often shrugged or responded, "I don't know." Student interviews were shorter than parent interviews, lasting approximately 10 to 20 minutes. In most cases students were interviewed at school.

Most students appeared to enjoy the interview process with the exception of Bradford, who had experienced a good deal of frustration with learning to read and was anxious to avoid any task related to reading.

Additional Interviews

Over the course of the yearlong research project, two parental figures, who were not focus parents, described themselves as being unable to read; both readily agreed to being interviewed about their experiences.

Classroom Data

Over the course of the research project, three types of classroom data were collected: audiotapes of class discussions; audiotapes of guided reading groups; and student-written documents, including student portfolios and journals.

Approximately twice a week, from September through June, I audio-taped our morning class discussions. Morning class discussions lasted approximately 15 minutes. We began each morning with a class meeting at which students discussed pertinent issues related to school, home, or community. Some discussions focused on reading strategies or purposes for reading, others on inquiry topics being explored by the class. The following is a typical discussion in which the children are talking about what they can do when they get stuck on a word while reading:

> *Seana:* Go back and try it.
> *Ms. Lilly:* OK, go back and try it. What else can you do?
> *Leshanda:* Ask a friend.
> *Javon:* Try the first letters.
> *Ms. Lilly:* Try the first letters.
> *Peter:* Just don't turn the page, just go back and use the sounds.
> *Ms. Lilly:* Good, you can try your sounds and try it again. Don't give up.
> *Christy:* Sound it out.
> *Ms. Lilly:* Sound it out. That's a hard one to do sometimes, but the first letter helps, doesn't it?
> *Alisa:* Look at the letters.
> *Jemon:* Look at the pictures.

Approximately 4 months into the research project, I became interested in ways the reading behaviors exhibited by students either did or did not reflect student and parent beliefs about student reading behaviors. I began to audiotape guided reading groups (Pinnell & Fountas, 1996) once or twice a week. Tapes from the guided reading groups include not only examples of students reading in groups and in pairs but also student discussions that precede and follow the reading of a new book. After reading a story about a lion and a mouse, we discussed the problem in the story:

Ms. Lilly: Who can tell me how they solved the problem?
Tiffany: At the end they were friends.
Ms. Lilly: Why? What happened to make them friends?
Ariana: The mouse helped the lion.
Ms. Lilly: And Tanya, how did the mouse help the lion?
Tanya: Because he wanted to help everything.
Ms. Lilly: And what did he do to help them?
Tanya: Get him out of the trap?
Jermaine: He nibbled and nibbled.

Student-written documents were also collected and analyzed. These included individual and group student writing (journal entries, stories and books that reflect the topic of literacy, questionnaires about literacy for parents and other audiences) as well as completed portfolios. Student portfolios included student text levels as determined by the "text level" portion of the Observation Survey (Clay, 1993); these were collected three times during the school year. Text level assessments were used to ascertain the reading level of each student.

Field Notes

As a teacher-researcher, I kept daily field notes; initially, these were designed to document my perceptions of my students as readers and the research process. In retrospect, I was surprised to discover that the bulk of these field notes focused on political aspects of teaching at Rosa Parks School and our status as a school in performance review. My field notes reflected issues such as district philosophy and mandates, the instructional materials provided, the basal textbook pilot program, my reaction to literacy practices in other classrooms, administrative support and expectations, literacy training sessions, school attempts to encourage parental involvement, and successful and unsuccessful implementations of various literacy practices.

The following is a typical entry. This one focuses on a PTA meeting that was mandated by the State Education Department to collect parent input on barriers that were preventing our students from learning to read.

The people from the coalition [a local activist group that supports many Puerto Rican families at our school] seemed to be annoyed at the format [of the meeting] and the process the facilitator was using. I guess the format came from the state, but the facilitator was very careful to record people's words accurately. However, the process stifled tangential conversation that may have been significant. For example, if one parent raised an issue about communication and another raised a similar issue, the facilitator would ask the second parent to wait until [all] three columns of the chart were completed by the first parent. In some cases, I could see very clear connections between the two issues. The process of filling in all three columns took at least 15 minutes per question and made it so that in the hour and 45 minutes only four issues were raised.

An hour and 45 minutes into the meeting, I went to take Carly [my daughter] to the bathroom, and when I returned [the school principal] was saying something like, "Oh boy, that's a big one." (Jokingly.) You wait until a quarter to 8 to raise that?" Apparently a parent had identified teachers as an obstacle to [children] learning to read. [The principal] invited parents to speak about that. They referred to teachers not knowing the children, [teachers] asking kids to wait [instead of helping them when they need help], and [teachers] not knowing what they are doing. Not much else was said but the idea was recorded along with the others.

As I began this research project, it was not my intent that my field notes would reflect evolving political disputes over curriculum, pedagogy, and parent involvement; however, the degree to which these disputes pervade my field notes attests to the consuming role these issues played in my school life during this particularly stressful year. Furthermore, the field notes illustrate the types of concerns that often consume urban teachers and administrators, preventing school staff from exploring other issues and working toward becoming responsive and sensitive to the communities in which they work.

ANALYSIS OF DATA

Data analysis began immediately following the first interviews and continued throughout the data collection process as emerging themes were shared with participants and new information was collected. Across interviews and among speakers, different explanations of issues related to reading emerged.

The actual analysis process began with transcription of the data. Audiotapes were transcribed in full with the exception of interruptions and salutary conversation. On two occasions, parents asked me to turn off the tape so that they could share with me information that they felt might incriminate them in some way. These comments were related to information that they preferred not to risk being shared with social service agencies or were remarks they made about a particular individual at Rosa Parks School. Such comments were not included in the data sample.

Coding was completed according to the grounded theory model of Strauss and Corbin (1990). In this model three types of coding (open coding, axial coding, and selective coding) are used to identify pertinent themes and to develop a contextualized model of the process of learning to read. Each of the following four chapters focuses on a theme that was identified through the coding processes. These themes include the roles of reading, supporting young readers, personal relationships that form around reading, and reading identities. Critical discourse analysis procedures as described by Norman Fairclough (1989, 1993, 1995) were used extensively to analyze and situate data.

Critical Discourse Analysis

> My view is that "discourse" is the use of language seen as a form of social practice, and discourse analysis is analysis of how texts work within sociocultural practice. Such analysis requires attention to textual form, structure, and organization at all levels; phonological, grammatical, lexical (vocabulary), and higher levels of textual organization in terms of exchange systems (the distribution of speaking turns), structures of augmentation, and generic (activity type) structures. (Fairclough, 1995, p. 7)

Throughout this book, I will analyze data in the manner that Fairclough describes. Sometimes I note the grammatical structures participants use; at other times I focus on vocabulary or the means by which people express their ideas. As Fairclough (1989) explains, any text can be analyzed on three dimensions: the contents of that text, the language used to express that content, and the ways subjects are positioned through the expression of that text. Thus, the words of my students and their parents not only reveal their perspectives and convey information, but also relay additional information via the terms they adapt and adopt to express their ideas and reveal how they position themselves within the stories they tell (Fairclough, 1989).

The analysis of texts, including spoken language, "is better able than other methods to capture sociocultural processes in the course of their occurrence, in all their complex, contradictory, incomplete, and messy materiality" (Fairclough, 1995, p. 186). Thus, as I try to understand how the reading experiences of my students and their parents are situated within their personal lives and school experiences, discourse analysis provides me with a methodological tool for revealing the process by which multiple discourses intersect within the lives of my students and their families. Discourse analysis has the potential to reveal contradictions between various ideological positions and power struggles that permeate the lives of teachers, students, and parents. These contradictions can be difficult to identify and examine. As Sarah Carney explains:

> Researchers must be willing to look deeply (and over the long term) into particular spaces in order to begin to find evidence of alternative discourses—especially if they are looking for language that runs counter to deeply held cultural beliefs. (2000, p. 135)

For me as a teacher-researcher concerned about simplistic and ungrounded explanations for the reading difficulties of my students, discourses analysis provides a means to uncover alternative interpretations of what constitutes learning to read in this urban community.

Fairclough (1989) offers lists of questions that researchers can use to explore and situate texts within larger political and social contexts. These questions focus on linguistic features of texts as well as conventions of interaction, control over textual events, and whose voices are included or excluded. I have applied these to texts gathered throughout the data analysis process to understand not only the meanings conveyed through these texts but also how the speaker is situated with larger social and political contexts. Because discourse analysis focuses on the precise words and phrasings of speakers, I have made the decision to leave all participant quotes in their original form. I trust that readers will recognize the imperfections of all spoken language irrespective of the speaker's dialect or social class.

BEING A TEACHER-RESEARCHER

As a teacher, I have the goal to acknowledge, respect, and build upon the multiple realities that my students and their families bring to school; as a researcher I strive to capture these realities on paper. As a teacher-researcher, I cannot accept simplified cause and effect explanations for the realities and experiences of my students, nor can I accept the reduction of our classroom world or local community to a numerical, codified description. Understanding complex questions about the intersections of reading and people's lives requires rich qualitative methods that present information in its complete and lived essence. I aim to explore the complex and often contradictory perspectives that my students and their parents present in order to examine the concepts of reading that are expressed by them.

I inhabit the physical world of the classroom and play a significant role in creating that community. However, because I am an outsider to my students' home communities, it is problematic for me to assume that I understand their reality, their values, and their conceptions about reading. I cannot assume that I share the perspectives, insights, and values of the community; my perspective may not reflect "their time and space" (Burawoy, 1991, p. 291). As a teacher, I am faced with the challenge of designing curricula and experiences that will help my students learn to read; thus, I value becoming responsive to the ideas, words, and insights of my students, their families, and their community.

Associated with being both my students' teacher and a researcher is the concern that parents and children may have provided me with the responses that they felt I wanted to hear. Although this danger is real, I do not believe that this was typically the case. The parents I interviewed were remarkable in the strength and thoughtfulness of their responses. They often challenged me, corrected me, and clarified their thoughts for me. Because we had spent months together in the classroom talking about reading, most children had a fairly good idea of my views on reading. While in some cases I did hear my own words being spoken back to me by students, in most cases mainstream discourses rather than the discourses of the teacher and the classroom were expressed by children. For example, my diligent young students talk about "sounding out" words. However, because many words in English are not phonetic and children tend to isolate each sound in sequence rather than linking the sounds together, I encourage students to attend to the beginnings, endings, and middles of words as well as to look through words; I consciously avoid using the phrase *sound it out* in the classroom. However, in interviews with children, they consistently spoke about sounding out words. Thus, it was the lack of my own teacher voice that struck me rather than its presence.

BEING A WHITE TEACHER

Eight years ago, when I first taught at Rosa Parks School, I was immediately aware of the cultural and racial differences between myself and the school community. I was White, my students were African American and Puerto Rican. While I made many mistakes during my first years at this school, I found wonderful mentors both on the staff and in the community who pointed out my errors and assumptions and encouraged me despite my failings. I did not consider myself a particularly effective teacher; test scores were low and I did not feel that my students were learning to read particularly well. However, parents recognized my interest in children and often requested me as their child's teacher, and I began to be assigned the children (and parents) that other teachers could not handle.

However, throughout this time I continued to struggle with my role of being both White and the teacher. It bothered me that the only White person in the room was the one responsible for deciding how things would run. With the help of staff members, particularly custodial staff, paraprofessionals, and cafeteria assistants who lived in the community, I began to find a comfortable role. However, I continue to engage in dialogue with colleagues and struggle to remain sensitive to the interests of parents and children.

Weis (1992) makes recommendations to researchers who conduct studies in communities of which they are not members. Weis recommends that researchers know who they are before going into the field, acknowledge their perspective, respect those with whom they work, and conduct themselves with the utmost integrity at all times. As a teacher, I have tried to apply these recommendations to my teaching over the past 12 years. Attaining success in this venture will be a lifelong challenge. As Marilyn Cochran-Smith explains:

> Attempting to make the unending process of unlearning racism explicit and public is challenging and somewhat risky. Easily susceptible to misinterpretation and misrepresentation, going public involves complex nuances of interpretation, multiple layers of contradiction, competing perspectives, and personal exposure. (2000, p. 158)

Despite a school discourse that blames parents for the difficulties of students, I have tried to withhold judgment about students and parents by listening carefully to the messages parents and students convey—both spoken and unspoken. However, arguments that blame parents can be very convincing and reassuring to a teacher concerned about efficacy; moreover, claims made in defense of parents are difficult to substantiate and sustain.

CONCLUSION

I did not begin this project with the goal of completing a discourse analysis that would demonstrate how a range of theoretical concepts play out in the words and lives of my students and their families. However, analysis of this data led me to an awareness that the people I interviewed were accessing discourses that were often contradictory.

In this book, I analyze the data not only to understand the ways my students and their families understand and make sense of reading but also to explore how their words contribute to the ongoing construction of both mainstream and alternative discourses. I will explore the hegemony of mainstream discourses that exists despite participants' simultaneous invocation of alternative discourses that contradict mainstream ways of thinking. I will also examine how alternative ways of thinking about and explaining the world are silenced and controlled. Social resources that participants access and draw upon (Fairclough, 1995) as well as what these data reveal about the experience of learning to read in my school community will be explored. Of critical interest is how these discourses are used and abandoned within a social field in which racism, poverty, and low levels of institutionally recognized cultural capital intersect.

3

The Role of Reading in the Lives of My Students and Their Families

Ms. Rodriguez: I think everybody needs to learn how to read, really, cuz I don't think you're really going to survive in this world without reading. You know.

Ms. Lilly: Not easily.

Ms. Rodriguez: And [with the ability to read] it's still not going to [fades out] be [easy] . . .

Ms. Rodriguez is adamant that learning to read is important; learning to read is more than useful and more than necessary for gaining employment or access to resources; Ms. Rodriguez equates learning to read with "survival." None of the parents whom I interviewed questioned the importance of learning to read, and their words often echoed Ms. Rodriguez's as they associated reading and "survival."

James Gee describes "pervasive social theories" (1990, p. 139) that circulate through society yet generally remain unquestioned and unexamined because of their naturalized and "taken for granted" status. These assumptions about the world include Ms. Rodriguez's claims about the necessity of learning to read. The importance of learning to read is part of a mainstream discourse that few people challenge. However, as mentioned in the introduction, Harvey Graff challenged this assumption on the basis of his historical study of literacy and social mobility. Graff wrote:

> Illiteracy could prove a great disadvantage to many, but not an insurmountable barrier to survival, adjustment or progress; conversely literacy and education did remarkably little in themselves to aid the greatest numbers in erasing ascriptive burdens, in canceling the disadvantages of their origins, or in gaining upward mobility. (1979, p. 191)

More recently, Patrick Shannon (1998) explores how literacy is often presented as a solution to poverty. However, as Shannon explains, increasing levels of literacy among poor people without attention to social, political, and economic inequities will fail to result in substantial and lasting gains.

Of importance in my research are the ways in which participants in this study understand the importance of reading and the role of reading in their lives. In this chapter, I will explore this relationship between reading and survival and present three constructs used by parents in associating reading with "getting somewhere." Finally, I will explore the manner in which children and parents describe people who cannot read.

READING AND SURVIVAL

Javon's mother shares Ms. Rodriguez's commitment to reading; speaking of her children, she says, "That's the only way they going to make it in life. They have to learn how to read." Ms. Horner, Ms. Mason, and Ms. Johnson agree:

> *Ms. Horner:* Yeah, um, I think of read[ing] as uh, uh, a daily function. You need to learn. You need to be able to read in order to be able to survive. It's definitely important.

> *Ms. Mason:* That's the only way they going to make it in life. They have to learn how to read.

> *Ms. Johnson:* You know, I always took reading for granted. But now, you know, I know you have to read in order to live.

The parents of my students use powerful language to emphasize the importance of learning to read ("need to," "survive," "make it in life"). The importance they place upon reading is not limited to employment opportunities or school success; these goals are not even mentioned in the examples above. The parents in this study associate reading with a range of real-life challenges, including "daily functions," "survival," and "in order to live." For the parents of my students, the need to read clearly extends beyond the classroom and workplace into everyday life.

During the course of this research project I spoke with Ariana's foster grandmother, Ms. Allan, who by her own account could read very little. She explained: "Reading and writing, you have to have those two things to get through the world today. You know what I mean? You can't get by without reading and writing. Mmm-mmm. I don't know what else to say." What is remarkable is that this comment accompanied a lengthy conversation with Ms. Allan about all the clever ways she has compensated for her lack of reading and writing skills; Ms. Allan dropped out of school in the fifth grade. Through her resourcefulness and resilience she managed to work several different jobs, including driving a school bus, until she recently went on disability. Although her life has certainly not been easy, she has proved herself very capable of getting "through the world" with only a minimal level of literacy. While verbally eliciting the dominant discourse that emphasizes the importance of reading, Ms. Allan's life challenges this discourse by describing the means by which she successfully maneuvered the world; however, her challenge remains couched within mainstream discourses about the absolute necessity of learning to read.

In sum, my students and their parents consistently describe reading as essential to survival; "there is reading no matter what you do." Even Ms. Holt, who explains, "I don't get into reading," insists that reading is extremely important for her son: "You're lost. If you can't read, you can't do anything." This association between reading and survival is part of a mainstream discourse that presents reading as absolutely essential.

READING AND "GETTING SOMEWHERE"

In our interviews, parents describe the relationship between reading and "getting somewhere" in three different ways. First and foremost, parents talk about getting somewhere in terms of a relationship between being able to read and securing viable employment. Second, parents view reading as necessary for physical mobility; they talk about the need to read for driving a car or even crossing the street. Third, parents describe getting somewhere in terms of letting their minds travel through a book. The associations that are made between reading and each of these means of getting somewhere suggest that reading presents multiple possibilities to urban families. While mainstream discourses about urban parents question their interest in reading and ability to read, the parents interviewed for this study emphatically describe reading as both extremely important and personally pleasurable.

"You Need to Get a Job"

When asked about the importance of learning to read, both parents and students commented extensively on the relationship between reading and employment. Consider the following comments:

Peter: [People who can't read] can't get a job then they won't get no money then no car or no house.

Ms. Horner: [People who can read] can follow directions [at work] a lot more better.

Alicia: You need to read because you need to get a job.

Ms. Webster: [If] you can't read, how are you going to fill out an application?

Interviews are saturated with comments that describe reading as essential for gaining employment and achieving economic success. These comments are offered with great confidence and at times polite amusement. Ms. Johnson replied with a smile that betrayed the obviousness of the answer to the question, "I would think so. I mean with any job you have these days you have to know how to read." Her amusement is understandable. I am teaching her child to read; I must surely recognize the importance of reading.

In other cases, statements about the relationship between reading and employment were strongly worded and intensely spoken. Consider this conversation with Ms. Hudson:

Ms. Hudson: 'Cause everyone need to learn how to read you know. Reading is the main subject, and the math.
Ms. Lilly: What does that mean in terms of his future?
Ms. Hudson: Mmm, him being a doctor, lawyer, teacher. You got to learn how to read and do math.

Ms. Hudson uses particularly strong language to express her beliefs about the importance of learning to read. Terms such as *everyone, need, got to,* and *the main subject* convey Ms. Hudson's conviction that learning to read is critical for gaining access to quality employment opportunities.

Ms. Webster shares Ms. Hudson's insistence that her child learn to read to get a job. To Ms. Webster, reading is central to the success-oriented scenario she describes for her daughters. She adamantly wants her children to become readers so that they can maneuver through college and job applications and get a job that pays a decent wage.

Anyway she looks at it you need to learn to read when you get a job. [If] you can't read then how are you going to fill out an application? And one thing I want her to do is get a job. I want her to go to college. I want my other daughter to go to college. Something that I never had. OK? And one thing I want them, both of them, to get a good education and get a good job and not have one of these penny-enny [jobs]. You know. You know.

Mr. Sherwood agrees. When I asked Mr. Sherwood if you could get a good job without reading skills, he expresses his frustration with low-paying jobs.

Not now. No 'cause you got, mainly you got too, too much, um, there's too much high tech. . . . The kids, um, they're not going to do uh garbage jobs. I call them garbage jobs. They not want, won't do it. Kids today will not want to do it, uh-uh. I'm not going to do that, not for that [amount of pay].

Mr. Sherwood recognizes that jobs are out there but that they often fail to pay a living wage. Thus, reading skills are associated with more than getting a job; they are associated with getting a *good* job.

My students also accepted an assumed relationship between learning to read and getting a job. Jasmine surprised me by answering a question that I thought would elicit a description of reading strategies used by good readers with a reference to employment.

Ms. Lilly: What things do good readers do?
Jasmine: Good readers do?
Ms. Lilly: Mmm-hmm, what do they do?
Jasmine: They go to jobs.

Jasmine's matter-of-fact response implies an assumed direct relationship between reading and employment as well as a different interpretation of my question.

David has a very clear understanding of what he believes happens to people who can't read.

David: They go and get fired.
Ms. Lilly: Anything else?
David: And then, and then the boss comes and picks another person to work for him.

Thus, reading is not only critical for getting a job; it is essential for maintaining a job. David certainly understands that without requisite reading skills employees are expendable and replacement personnel are always available.

"You're Lost If You Can't Read"

Ms. Holt shares her concerns about not knowing how to read:

> You're lost. If you can't read, you can't do anything. If you can't read you can't do math. You can't read you can't do science. You can't read, you can't even hardly walk cause you can't see a sign—"don't walk." You can't read it. You got to be able to do it.

In this short passage, Ms. Holt uses the word *can't* ten times. She mentions various academic subjects that she reports cannot be done without being able to read. Ms. Holt concludes her comments by explaining that without reading you cannot even read the signs to cross the street; you can't go anywhere or "do anything." Reading can help you get somewhere while people who cannot read are "lost."

Of the 10 parents interviewed, 7 spontaneously mentioned the importance of reading for driving a car. Ms. Rodriguez shared with me a conversation she had with a man who was taking adult reading classes at a local adult education center.

> One guy said he wanted to learn how to read because he had to learn to get around because he said a lot of times when you drive, you couldn't, he couldn't read the signs. So he was always lost and I was like I never thought of that. I really didn't; I never thought about, you know, when you're driving, even when you're traveling on a bus, anything, you got to read to ask [know] where you are going.

Mr. Sherwood is amazed by a man he knows who drives a truck but cannot read:

> I know people who drive a truck out here, you know, going back and forth to finish their route, they don't know, they don't know how to read a darn sign out there. It's really amazing . . . and you got kids playing around here, he came, and they can come around that corner like it ain't nothing. You know because they can't read.

Mr. Sherwood blames the truckers speeding around corners on his not being able to read yet there are no "slow children" signs around Mr. Sherwood's house. While logically, the speed of the trucks cannot be blamed on illiteracy, Mr. Sherwood suggests that if they could read they might not speed around corners; his assumption may be that being able to read is associated with particular qualities such as being conscientious, considerate, and law abiding.

Children also mentioned the importance of reading for driving. Javon explains that truck drivers "have to read what the owner [boss] of them put down on the paper [to] go to the next house." Jasmine described things that are important to read: "Umm, stop signs, like you don't look, you don't look where you are going; that's the sign so you stop." Peter was less clear on exactly what truck drivers have to read: "They read papers so they know how to drive."

"It Takes Your Mind Away"

Another manner in which parents associate reading with "getting somewhere" is through descriptions of reading as an escape from their everyday world. Unlike reading as a means for gaining employment or driving a car, reading as a means of escape reveals a nonutilitarian role of reading; it presents the importance of reading for personal reasons and enjoyment. Many parents shared intense and highly personal responses to books:

> *Ms. Mason:* Well, sometimes it just take[s] your mind away, a new adventure.

> *Ms. Webster:* [In reference to the "romance stories" she likes to read] it's the thrill, I don't know, it's like falling in love again.

> *Ms. Rodriguez:* It takes you to a different place. It relaxes you.

> *Ms. Horner:* I'm a dreamer and I like to let my mind imagine, [it] just takes me places I wish I could be.

Each of these responses focuses on reading as a means to explore new worlds and new experiences. Reading "takes your mind away" and "lets your mind imagine." Reading is both a "thrill" and relaxation. For these parents, reading is a means of escape from their everyday lives and an opportunity to travel within their minds. As their children's teacher, I had no clues that would have led me to realize that recreational reading was important in the lives of these particular parents. Parents did not reveal their enthusiasm about reading until I visited their homes and asked them directly about reading. While the mainstream discourses within my school suggest the opposite, I discovered that most of the parents I interviewed were avid readers. One mother described staying up late at night to finish a novel; another describes the animated conversations she has with her friends about books. A third mother goes into the kitchen to read when her boyfriend turns out the bedroom light. Still another mother describes herself as an enthusiastic reader of American history. Other parents regularly read the newspaper, "bingo books," and magazines.

Perhaps the most extensive description of the ways reading takes you places came from Ms. Green, who found reading to be a source of consolation while dealing with the ordeal of chronic bipolar disorder.

> Especially when I felt something was bothering me I would sit down and I would read. A lot of them were children's books. And they're mostly in the sixties they were written. Like uh, *Henry and the Club House.* You know that one. And I would be upset or something I would read those books and it would make me feel better. Also my mother would read to me. And when we were in North Carolina, I was having a lot of problems and we would read together, my father, my mother, and me out loud sometimes. We read *Gone With The Wind.* Out loud. OK?

Rereading favorite children's books helped Ms. Green to temporarily escape her problems and to feel better. Interestingly, she describes the close personal relationships that developed around reading as her family used reading to help her deal with mental illness.

The words of my students and their parents clearly demonstrate their perspective that reading is important for employment, mobility, and enjoyment. In the following section, I turn to participant descriptions of not knowing how to read.

NOT KNOWING HOW TO READ

The parents I interviewed challenged mainstream discourses as they describe people who do not know how to read. Rather than merely blaming the inability of people to read on personal failings, parental neglect, or low intelligence, many parents describe the inability to read as situated within particular sets of circumstances related to urban schools and life experiences. Several parents indicated that people who do not know how to read are generally "older folks" who never went to school or only went for a short time. Over the course of this research, I interviewed a child's great-grandmother and another child's foster grandmother who by their own accounts were unable to read. Both were older folks who had not completed elementary school. For these people, dropping out of school was necessary so that they could assist their families financially.

In discussions about younger people who do not learn to read, the explanations are very different. Participants agree that most young adult nonreaders either do not care about school or simply get "passed along" through school. Ms. Waterton, Jerome's great-grandmother, who herself left school in the sixth grade and reports that she cannot read except "a little bit," expressed great frustration with younger people who went to school but cannot read; her comments echo mainstream discourses that blame those who cannot read for their own illiteracy. She speaks vehemently about her 18-year-old granddaughter, who "don't go to school . . . don't know how to count . . . don't even [know] how to spell her own name" and "ain't trying to learn nothing." Ms. Waterton finds her own experience of not having had the opportunity to complete school very different from that of young people who have had the opportunity to attend school yet failed to learn to read.

Other parents point to the role schools play in children not learning to read. Half the parents in this sample explained that students get passed along through school without learning to read, although most parents report having no firsthand knowledge of this occurring. Parents cite the case of the high school athlete who is passed along so he can play sports. They explain that schools pass children along for quasi-commendable reasons, such as helping students to "get into the big league, I guess, to make money." While parents do not condone the school's actions, they do give the school credit for helping the child to achieve his or her athletic goals.

In contrast, Ms. Mason believes that the "school system [will] hurry up and pass" those kids who "stay in a lot of trouble" just to "try and get them out" of school. Here the schools are clearly not working on behalf of students; when schools pass children along to get them out of school, it is the school's interests that are paramount.

Whether it's because of athletics or because some students "stay in a lot of trouble," there is a shared understanding among the parents I interviewed that some children do get passed along without learning to read. This same belief is reported in a case study by Arlene Fingeret and Cassandra Drennon (1997), in which a research subject with low literacy skills reports, "I don't know how the hell I got that," referring to his high school vocational certificate. He suspects that he was given his certificate to get him out of the program.

Of the parents I interviewed, only Marvin's grandfather, Mr. Sherwood, reports firsthand knowledge of a person who was passed along:

I had um, real I have a friend, a dear friend of mine. He's real close in [a nearby city]. And he was in the same class I was in [where the teacher just put a book in front of him and told him to read]. Um he can, um he couldn't read at all. And, and um when it was time for us to pass schools, but um passing, um let me think, 11th grade, and they um passed him too and he couldn't read. Then in the summertime we'd get summer jobs. I had to fill his application out.

Mr. Sherwood believes that the educational system passed his friend along, all the way through high school, without ever attending to the fact that his friend could not read. What is missing from this account is any mention of why Mr. Sherwood's friend was passed along. There is no mention of athletics. The idea that his friend was not interested in school seems unlikely, since Mr. Sherwood goes on to describe this friend as being very good at math and a "great chess player" who had won several awards. Discourses that blame the inability of students to read on causing trouble or participating in school athletics fail to account for Mr. Sherwood's friend.

Children also talk about the possibility of not learning to read and the consequences it would have in their lives. Children speak emphatically about what happens to people who cannot read. I asked Christy what would happen if a grownup couldn't read:

Christy: They wouldn't know anything.
Ms. Lilly: Mmm-hmm, and then what would happen?
Christy: Then somebody would come to them and says do you know this word and they might not know it.
Ms. Lilly: Mmm-hmm, anything else happen?
Christy: If they give a book to him, they wouldn't know how to read? (voiced as if asking a question)
Ms. Lilly: You're right. And how, what would happen if they didn't know how to read?
Christy: Uh books.
Ms. Lilly: What would happen with the book?
Christy: They'd get old and couldn't read them.

Christy expresses dire consequences of not knowing how to read. People who cannot read not only embarrass themselves by not being able to read books and words, but they also "wouldn't know anything" and they would "get old and couldn't read" books. To Christy, not knowing how to read is a curse that results in an embarrassing state of ignorance and humiliation.

However, in some cases children do not recognize the fact that there may be people in their lives who cannot read. According to David's mother, David's father has very low reading skills. Throughout the interview process David showed no sign of being aware of his father's difficulties with reading even when asked directly if he knew anyone who did not read well.

Seven of the 10 focus students expressed concern that not being able to read is a potential source of embarrassment, especially within the public forum of the classroom. Jermaine relates, "If you go to second grade and the teacher [gives] you a book and the teacher tell you to read, if you say no, you don't know how to read." Alisa shares Jermaine's concerns: "You need to use the word and if you don't use the word, you won't learn the word and if you don't use the word, um, you might don't know how to read that good and people will laugh at you."

These children echo Christy's concern that not knowing how to read is humiliating and embarrassing. Children often associate not being able to read with being ridiculed. Within the peer group, attaining the ability to read is an accomplishment that demonstrates to the teacher and classmates that you are competent and capable.

Ms. Webster shares the children's concerns about making reading errors in front of peers. She describes her concerns about pronouncing words incorrectly in her adult job-skills class.

> Now there's some words in my books from school, you look at these words and it's like how do you pronounce it? And there could be several different ways to pronounce it. And then if you say it wrong, the teacher will correct you. Then it makes you look, I mean being my age, [it] makes you look stupid, OK?

Eight out of the 10 parents reported that they sometimes had difficulties "pronouncing words" correctly, and for several parents this was a major concern. As Mr. Sherwood reports, "Sometimes I get caught up on a word uh, um, I can't pronounce. And it affects, it affects you." He goes on to describe this as his reading "problem" even though he explains that he knows the word and it doesn't "mess up" his comprehension. This verbal display of reading, a school-valued skill, is important to both children and their parents. Furthermore, participants' concerns with getting laughed at reflect mainstream notions about literacy that view illiteracy as shameful.

While several children reported their fears of embarrassment at not being able to read, by far the biggest concern of first graders was the fear of not going to second grade. My students correctly recognize that reading is the primary factor in being promoted. When first-grade teachers at our school discuss retention, the child's reading ability is the major criterion. This emphasis on reading was magnified at my school, where discontinuation of the school's charter was threatened on the basis of our chronically low reading scores and our School in Performance Review status with the State Education Department.

When Marvin was asked why he felt that he needed to learn how to read, he replied, "So you can go to second grade." Marvin simply explains that learning to read means that you can progress to second grade. Marvin understands this well; he was retained last year based on his difficulties with reading. Learning to read is a defense against failure and is rarely described by my students as pleasurable, useful, or valuable based on its own merits.

Javon also understands the relationship between reading and promotion; when asked how he knew that learning to read was going well for him, he replied, "Because I'm getting into the grades." The fact that students view promotion as evidence of school success is particularly frightening when seen in relation to parents' contention that some children are passed along without attaining adequate academic achievement; the question of whether promotion is an accurate reflection of academic achievement is clearly raised.

James's words reflect a sense of foreboding; when asked why he needed to learn to read, he responded, "Because if you go to second grade and you [don't] know how to read they gonna put you back in kindergarten." James's use of the word *they* is particularly interesting. He views retention not only as a consequence of not being able to read but also as something that "they," those with power, do to children. However, "they" is actually me as well as other members of the school organization who make the decisions about which children will be promoted and which will be retained. James may have been reluctant to name me, his teacher, as among those responsible for the horrific act of sending children back to kindergarten.

CONCLUSION

This chapter opened with the words of Ms. Rodriguez and other parents who described knowing how to read as critical for survival. These parents unanimously attest to the importance of learning to read in the lives of their children. While social theorists have challenged the relationship between reading and social and economic mobility (Graff, 1979; Shannon, 1998), parents in this study continue to associate reading with gaining viable employment and mobility. This is one of the many mainstream discourses about reading that proliferate in our schools and society. Literacy is often identified as the quintessential cure for social ills and economic deprivation. By naming literacy as the ultimate tool to fight poverty and social oppression, schools and society can blame the poor for their own failings when scores of poor African American and Hispanic students, like those in my classroom, fail to demonstrate expected levels and appropriate types of literacy accomplishment despite successive years of formal education.

In closing, I will extrapolate from this chapter three mainstream discourses about reading that my students and their parents cite and connect these to some of the theoretical constructs presented in Chapter One.

Reading is a means to employment. Both parents and children attest to the importance of learning how to read for getting and keeping a good job. In Chapter Seven examples of parents challenging this mainstream discourse will be presented.

Not knowing how to read is a personal failing. Several parents criticized young people who could not read as lazy while older folks are often recognized as not having had the opportunity to finish school; parents also explained that schools "pass on children" without ensuring that children have learned to read.

Not being able to read is a source of embarrassment. Both parents and children voiced concern that not knowing how to read or even how to pronounce a particular word correctly is embarrassing.

All these discourses were cited by the parents of my students. As Fairclough (1989) maintains, mainstream discourses generally become naturalized and often remain unquestioned even when evidence to the contrary is presented. Luke (1995b) explains that presenting a particular way of seeing the world as common sense establishes and maintains the hegemony of particular ideologies and the institutions that support them. This explains how the same speaker can blame individuals for not knowing how to read while also accusing the school of passing students along without teaching them to read. The dominance of the mainstream discourse relegates alternative explanations to the margins.

It must be remembered that literacy instruction in schools subjects people to conformity in the ways they read, write, speak, act, and interact. It defines "appropriateness" in terms of what is "appropriate" for those in power (Fairclough, 1993), denying alternative ways of reading, writing, speaking, acting, and interacting while penalizing people whose linguistic and cultural backgrounds do not align with established norms; these are often people whose race, class, or home language patterns differ from those of mainstream society. The discourses presented in this chapter clearly articulate to my students and their families that learning to read is immensely important for both survival and employment and that failure to read is both a personal failing and a source of embarrassment. Alternative ways of understanding reading are silenced, and challenges to mainstream ways of thinking are often couched as an aside to mainstream interpretations and offered with hesitancy.

Analysis of the data in this study has been used to create a contextualized model of reading and learning to read. Figures 3.1 and 3.2 explore tensions between mainstream and alternative discourses. Figure 3.1 reflects generally accepted interpretations of the existing social, economic, and political context and reflects the interests of particular groups of

Figure 3.1. Generally Accepted Interpretations of the World

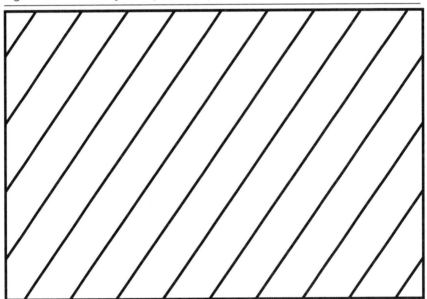

Figure 3.2. Alternative Discourses Collide With Mainstream Discourses

Alternative / Mainstream Discourses	Mainstream Discourses

people broadly based on race, class, and gender; in American society this is generally the interests of people who are Caucasian, middle and upper class, and male. Figure 3.2 presents both mainstream discourses and alternative discourses that challenge and run counter to these mainstream discourses. Subjects in this study reference both mainstream and alternative discourses; thus, there are times when their interpretations of reality mesh with mainstream interpretations, while at other times, alternative interpretations of reality grounded in people's lived experiences disrupt and challenge these mainstream discourses.

In the following chapter, additional mainstream and alternative discourses about reading will be revealed along with an additional component of this contextualized model of reading. Specifically, in Chapter Four I begin to explore the social relationships that surround reading and learning to read.

4

Parents' and Teachers' Roles in Helping Children Learn to Read

A few months before he entered my class, Marvin came to live with his grandparents; he was repeating first grade. At the end of our year together, his grandfather chuckled as he explained how Marvin's grandmother worked to get Marvin on track with reading. As he reports:

> She really packed it down on him. . . . His grandmother is really good. I mean she did a job on him. Cuz he didn't want nothing [to do with reading] but she say "Marvin, come here. Marvin! Come here!" And she really did a good job on him.

With the help of his grandmother, who "stayed on" him throughout the year, Marvin was reading at grade level by June. Based on my research, Marvin's grandmother is not unique among urban parents. Many urban parents are working hard to ensure that their children are successful in school.

Many researchers (Gordon, 1993; Lawrence-Lightfoot, 1978; Winters, 1993) have documented and criticized the tendency of urban teachers to severely judge the parents of their students. While this tendency can be viewed as merely an extension of mainstream discourses that degrade and devalue the contributions of urban residents, these discourses are not harmless. They position children and their families in ways that make it very difficult for educators to see beyond these assumptions and to recognize the many positive contributions that urban families make in supporting their children as readers. As Susan Hill and her colleagues explain, "When teachers have greater knowledge and respect for their students, they will construct an inclusive community which explicitly builds on children's existing cultural capital and preferred ways of learning" (1998, p. 11).

Stereotypes portray urban parents as uncaring and unconcerned; as will be demonstrated in this chapter, however, urban parents and students place a high value on reading. In the first part of this chapter, I will explore the various ways parents help their children with the task of learning to read. In the second part of the chapter, I will explore one particular type of support that was repeatedly mentioned by parents: parents spoke about the need to "stay on" their children throughout the research project.

PARENTS AS TEACHERS

The parents of my students express a great deal of interest in their children and particularly in their children's success with learning to read. Parents firmly believe that their children are smart. Mr. Sherwood describes the children in this community: "You know you got a lot of very smart kids in this neighborhood, very smart. I'm not talking about streetwise, I'm talking about *they is smart*" (Mr. Sherwood's emphasis). Ms. Holt recognizes intelligence overlooked by others: "All these peoples in jail . . . at least some of them who's in jail are gifted."

Parents in this study believe their children to be capable of academic achievement and seek ways to support their children with school-related tasks ranging from reading with children to providing educational games and materials. One student's mother insists that her daughter keeps the television on closed caption whenever she watches it, to help her learn to read. Other parents have purchased or are considering the purchase of computers and audiotape programs designed to help children develop phonics or math skills. Similarly, Ms. Holt reports that her mother purchased a variety of educational products for her and her siblings when they were growing up:

> *Ms. Lilly:* What did she [your mother] do to help you?
> *Ms. Holt:* Dick, Jane, and Sally . . .
> *Ms. Lilly:* She had them at home?
> *Ms. Holt:* . . . and Spot. Yes she had. And you know what else worked, that ARA [SRA, Scientific Research Associates] . . . Now it's Hooked on Phonics. But there were yellow, blue, green, purple—the purple was the advanced. But you started with the red and blue.

Ms. Holt believes that her mother still has these reading comprehension materials in her basement. Similarly, Ms. Mack describes some of the resources she uses to help her children:

The parents got to stay on their kids. And I, you know they have educational programs that come on television. Sesame Street . . . it's good for kids. And like, you know, they got all different kinds of educational toys coming out. And I think that I definitely do get kids a toy they can learn, benefit from.

Parents also create games that reinforce learning to read. Ms. Rodriguez describes a game she played with her children when they were in pre-school: "It's like when you say this is a window and you spell *window* and then you spell *door* and stuff like that. It's simple but as they grow up they be looking at it like, I learned how to read early. Yeah and I learned how to spell early." Ms. Rodriguez feels that these games helped her children learn how to spell words and to be successful with readinglike tasks at an early age.

Ms. Johnson also describes encouraging children to sound out unknown words as they read:

He'll get stuck on a word and he gets really annoyed. You know, "I don't know. I don't know." And I'm like "David, sound it out. You know your letters, you know the sounds. All you have to do is put them together and you'll know the word."

Of the 10 parents interviewed, 8 parents spontaneously reported that they encourage children to sound out words when they encounter difficulty. Like Ms. Johnson, several parents confess to a degree of frustration when children experience difficulties with sounding out words.

When parents describe helping their children learn words and letters, the practices they adopt generally resemble school reading practices and reflect mainstream assumptions about how children learn to read and write. About half the parents describe having children write words that they have trouble with; for example, Ms. Johnson asks David to write challenging words five times, "so he remembers [them]." Ms. Holt explains, "Because if you write it over and over you learn it." Writing out words, along with learning conventional spellings, and sounding out words reflect mainstream discourses about reading that emphasize reading as recognizing, memorizing, and decoding words. These practices also reflect standard educational practices that were common when parents attended school.

However, parents are not merely products of mainstream discourses and past practices. Throughout the interviews, they discuss reading in sophisticated terms. Mr. Sherwood aptly describes people who "word call"; they read the words on the page but do not understand what they are reading.

> You know, like a lot of people read it but they don't understand what they read, you know . . . they just read the whole paragraph and then when you ask them a, uh, whether um, what they read about, [they] don't even know that.

Other parents distinguish between reciting predictable books from memory and reading. Ms. Holt points to a simple predictable book that Bradford is reading on the floor nearby. It is a book that I sent home several weeks earlier.

> No, no, not, I'm not just saying [just] that book. I'm not saying any-thing's wrong with that book. Don't get me wrong, but I'm just saying that if he could read, you have to learn, know how to read before you can, see he memorizes that. Which is what I'm saying. That's not wrong, but he, if he sees that word . . . OK, he sees the word *cat* somewhere else is he going to know that word *cat*? With-out knowing [seeing it in] that book?

She goes on to explain: "If he sees that word, he should know it anywhere." Ms. Rodriguez makes a similar distinction. "Alisa focus on not sounds but memory. So she needs to get the sounds too. Not only just memorizing it." Parents recognize the dangers of simply memorizing text; they fear that if children rely only on aural memory to read, they will not be able to "read" the words in other contexts. Parents believe that children should be able to read words on sight. They want to know that their child knows words well enough that they will recognize them in any context.

On the basis of their research in Lancaster, England, Barton and Hamilton (1998) explain that the strategies people used to help others with reading appear to be grounded in their experiences. These strategies include

> a combination of ones they themselves had learned at school, ver-nacular ones they had learned at home, and ones they had them-selves invented. They drew upon their own experiences of what had helped them remember things, and also upon stereotypes of how teachers act and their images of school practices. (1998, p. 197)

The parents whom I interviewed also referenced multiple contexts for the strategies they use to help their children with reading. Some strategies such as sounding out words and writing challenging words were probably adapted from practices that parents had learned when they were in school, while Ms. Rodriguez invented spelling games to help her children learn. Other practices such as purchasing educational games may be connected to various advertising strategies targeted at parents (Shannon, 2001).

As mentioned in the introduction to this book, two of the parents of my students are the children of teachers; two others teach in preschool classrooms. I had never considered the wealth of experience and information that parents who work in preschools bring to the learning experiences of their children. Unfortunately, their contributions go unrecognized by teachers when urban parents are assumed to be uninformed, uninterested, and uninvolved.

In the following section, the words of parents will be used to explore how parents "stay on" children to ensure that children learn in school.

STAYING ON CHILDREN

In addition to parents' efforts to help children with the academic tasks involving reading, parents also report the need to "stay on" children. Parents explain that staying on children demonstrates caring and high expectations for children. Staying on children also reveals the intensity with which urban parents care about their children's success in learning to read. However, while 9 of the 10 parents interviewed described the ways they stay on their children, parents in this study also tended to criticize others in the community for neglecting their children or for failing to monitor their children's activities: "All these kids are running around . . . they don't do their homework," and "They take care of themselves all day long." This contradiction between what parents often report happening in their own homes and what happens in the homes of their neighbors again reveals the dominance of mainstream discourses and how even within the urban community these discourses prevail.

In this section, I will explore the importance parents place on staying on their children. I will then explore parents' own histories and the manner in which their teachers and parents monitored them when they were in school. Finally, I will present the words of my students as they describe their expectations for teachers.

"We Got to Stay on the Child"

Parents spontaneously described the importance of "staying on" their children. While parents expressed this idea in various ways, their intent remained the same. Parents reported "staying behind kids," not "giving up on kids," "cramping down" on them, "getting on" them, and letting them "know who's the boss." From the parents' perspective, *staying on kids* is definitely a positive expression. It shows children that parents care and will go out of their way to demonstrate their caring. Some parents report having their children watch educational television or read books; others describe not accepting sloppy or incorrect schoolwork. Parents who keep kids "on track," don't let them "go too far" and "don't give too much freedom." They report not "allowing it" and not "having it." These descriptions may appear tough and insensitive; however, the apparent contradiction between caring about a child and cramping down on him or her is erased when careful monitoring of children, and subsequent consequences, are interpreted as evidence of caring.

To my students' parents, keeping a child "on track" is essential to sustaining a nurturing and caring relationship. Parents describe other parents who do not monitor their children and do not enforce consequences as not caring about their children. Ms. Hudson, Jermaine's mother, describes these parents with a tone of exasperation:

> For one thing, they [children] might come in from school and, and come on in and drop off their books or coat or whatever and just go on inside. You know. And not even ask their parents or nothing just go on, go on outside and play. That's a parent that don't care. OK? That's a parent that don't care.

Ms. Hudson, like most people in our society, voices mainstream discourses that blame parents for the failings of their children. Parents often simultaneously criticize their neighbors, stating: "Their [the children's] parents aren't helping them" and "I don't think they [people in the community] read. Nobody reads." The dominance of mainstream discourses about the reading practices of urban families prevails even within the same local community that often falls victim to these discourses.

In contrast to myths and stereotypes about urban parents that imply that parents are lazy or do not care, the parents I interviewed describe monitoring and addressing their own children's behavior and attitude as an active and ongoing challenge.

Parents actively strive to keep children on track. They closely monitor

their children's behavior, present consequences, and enforce those consequences. Ms. Rodriguez credits herself with helping her 16-year-old son:

> *Ms. Rodriguez:* He started going into that stage where "I'm not go-
> ing to listen to you. I'll listen to everybody else except you."
> And I was like, "OK, so you don't want to listen to me? You
> stay in the house for a month." And then he like, "What? a
> month!" Who, um but that didn't do no good, so I said "OK,
> let's see how you like staying in the house for the whole sum-
> mer." . . . I say, "I'm just as stubborn as you. No!"
>
> *Ms. Lilly:* Wow.
>
> *Ms. Rodriguez:* So he stayed here for the whole summer. He cried.
> You got to look at him cry. [Laughs] And I'd sit here looking
> at him.
>
> *Ms. Lilly:* How's he doing now?
>
> *Ms. Rodriguez:* Now? B student. Back on track.

As Ms. Rodriguez explains, her role as a parent entails active participation
and demanding interactions that require tenacity and the will to persevere
despite frustration. Staying on a child entails a contest of wills with the
parent stubbornly pursuing success. Hugh Mehan noted a similar attitude
in his work with African American parents. He writes that "violations of
academic expectations were punished by restrictions, and the punish-
ments stuck" (1992, p. 9).

Ms. Mason faces similar challenges with her first-grade son, Javon.
As Javon's teacher I can attest to the fact that Javon's behavior in class
can be taxing. His mother expresses her frustration. "Take Javon for
example. I tried everything [with not much success]. So I say I'm not
going to give up on him." In a later interview, she explains, "Javon,
he's going to be someone very . . . he's going to make something very
important. I can [tell] because I am not going to give up on him." Parents
are stubborn and will not give up even when children challenge their
tenacity.

Staying on children applies not only to monitoring school behavior
and progress; Ms. Mason describes having high standards for her son's
schoolwork:

> 'Cause a lot of time when he writes and stuff, I don't like the, how
> his writing turn out. Then I go back and erase it. Sometimes he get
> upset but I don't. I tell him, I said well I wouldn't accept those
> papers that he get home sometimes. I tell him, I said, I wouldn't

accept that. If I was your teacher, I would not accept this paper, I said. Because you supposed to have a neat paper.

Other parents report keeping children inside the home or closely monitoring their actions when they go out. Ms. Holt explains that when her older children were growing up she was very concerned about their safety; she speaks with a sadness in her voice, wondering whether she had denied them something by keeping them so close:

> Ten years ago I wouldn't even let my children out alone without me going with them. And I call myself living in an area where it wasn't no gang, but then when they go to the store, hoodlums are on the corner. But when they go down the street to play with their friends, one of them [the hoodlums] be waiting. So I hibernated them [the kids] which wasn't good.

By closely monitoring her children, Ms. Holt clearly demonstrates caring for her children; yet in retrospect she wonders if she may have gone too far. Ms. Holt spent a significant amount of time during our interviews searching for answers to explain the difficulties her older children have faced as they grew up. In particular, the tragic death of her oldest son in a DWI (driving while intoxicated) accident has haunted her. She wonders if perhaps "hibernating" them "wasn't good." Parents describe staying on children as demanding a delicate balance between caring, careful monitoring, and allowing children just the right amount of freedom.

The fact that the parents I interviewed care deeply about the academic progress of their children is betrayed by the obvious passion and intensity with which parents talk about the need to stay on their children. Ms. Rodriguez adamantly insists that her high school-age sons get their diplomas:

> Oh, I stay on them and my son knows that I don't care if he didn't go to college. That's one thing but he says he probably end up going to trade school or something. I think that's fine. But one thing I've always told him. Regardless of what you do in life, you gonna have a diploma. I don't care what you do. You gonna bring home the diploma. And they all know that. And they all, come, they all you know, "Ma ain't going to let up 'til we get the diploma, so let's get it and get it over with."

Ms. Rodriguez agrees that the passion she expresses about her children bringing home a diploma is explained by the struggles she faced as a mother of six when she completed her GED. Ms. Rodriguez's words demonstrate caring but also tenacity and a sense of necessity. She's not going to "let up"; it is her responsibility to make sure her children get their diplomas.

Parents contrast staying on a child with allowing the child to "play." Ms. Hudson describes her efforts to get Jermaine to do his homework as soon as he comes home from school. She explains that this is a challenge, since "he be wanting to play when he comes in." But playing is not limited to childlike interactions with toys or friends. Playing is defined here as the failure to focus on academic tasks. Ms. Mason clearly contrasts playing with learning:

> We [parents] got to stay on the child. Because if you don't stay on them they love to play. They'll play around and they don't care. . . . If I could just get Javon to stop clowning around and distracting the class. I don't know why he always do that in her [the math teacher's] class.

Drawing on her own experiences, Ms. Webster explains that she "failed first grade" because "I didn't want to learn. I wanted to play." While parents recognize the tendency for children to want to "play," they do not allow this to be an excuse for failure to meet academic and behavioral expectations. There is no mention of waiting for the child to mature or lowering expectations. Children are expected to rise to the occasion and perform as required. Although some parents, like Ms. Mason, realize that getting Javon to change his behavior may take time, parents believe that if they stay on the child in a way that is both demanding and caring, the child will be successful.

"She Was a Great Teacher"

The parents I spoke with also believe that teachers need to stay on their students. Over the course of our interviews, almost every parent described a teacher who positively influenced them as they were coming through school. Teachers are not valued for simply being kind or compassionate. As Delpit (1995) and Ladson-Billings (1994) report, memorable teachers demand a lot from students but also care deeply about both the students and their academic progress.

Caring teachers demonstrate concern for their students in many obvious ways. Some teachers of participating parents invited students to stay at their homes; others made visits to students' homes. Caring teachers used games in the classroom to make learning fun and exciting. They "get into it with the students." Ms. Horner describes her second-grade teacher: "She just looked after me, um, made me feel real special." However, these demonstrations of caring are accompanied by high expectations for both academic progress and behavior.

A caring teacher is "tough" and "strict," but she cares, and the students "love her for it." The teacher demonstrates high expectations that are accompanied by a warm and nurturing relationship. Ms. Mason describes a teacher who she felt really cared:

> I used to tell my kids about this teacher I had when I was in about eighth grade. She was the type of person that if you didn't learn nothing, she not going to let you pass. Before any kid leave out of her class that kid learned how to read. And that showed the kids right then that she really cared, cause some teachers they don't care. And this lady I'm talking about her name was Ms. Downs and she was a great teacher . . . cause she stayed on you. If she figured that you were playing around and stuff she'll let you get away with it for a while, then she'll tell you straight up, hey you gonna learn before you leave out of my classroom . . . but every kid that went through her [class], they did learn.

Mr. Sherwood provides a similar description of one of his teachers. However, Mr. Sherwood's teacher used physical tactics to control students. While certainly a questionable practice in schools, Ms. Sherwood interprets this teacher's physical means as demonstrating to students that she cares.

> Ms. Collins, my teacher was strict too. She was. But she, she um teach them. Plus she was the principal too, you know. And, then, at that time, in my, at that time they, they discipline a kid. The way they got it now in schools, you know, and she didn't tell me to go stand in a corner. Now [back then] you don't go stand in a corner. They do things. They hit you and say now this is what you're going to learn and stuff, but they love her for it.

Being strict but caring also entails having confidence in student abilities and high expectations for students. Ms. Holt describes her third-grade teacher as being "hard" but also having confidence in the students' abilities:

> She was hard, I mean she was hard! But she, she was one, she was one, she was one of those teachers you gonna do it, you gonna do

it. There's not no, "I'm not going to hear the [words] *you can't*." *Can't*, I don't believe *can't* was in her vocabulary. You can and you will.

Like the successful teachers of African American children that Gloria Ladson-Billings identified as "conductors," these teachers demonstrate faith in their students' ability: "Conductors believe that students are capable of excellence and they assume responsibility for ensuring that their students achieve that excellence" (1994, p. 23). Similarly, Lisa Delpit describes the "authoritative teacher" who "establishes meaningful interpersonal relationships that garner student respect; exhibits a strong belief that all students can learn; establishes a standard of achievement and 'pushes' the students to achieve that standard" (1995, pp. 35–36).

However, not all teachers convey faith in students' abilities and a sense of caring. Ms. Holt distinguishes tough, caring teachers from teachers who just don't care:

> Some teachers give uh, give their all to help these children. But some teachers they just . . . [pause; Ms. Holt imitates the teacher] "I'm here, I'm here, you're here and so hell, I'll have um, I'm, I'm going to get paid whether you do it or not." . . . You know because in my travels I've, I've ran into teachers, some teachers that gave me that attitude. . . . I didn't care for those teachers.

Mr. Sherwood agrees. He says that for "too many [teachers] it's like a, a job to them." He goes on to explain that these teachers do not take time with their students and thus fail to develop the kinds of relationships that demonstrate caring.

"My Mother Wouldn't Allow It."

Parents describe their own parents staying on them in much the same ways they describe staying on their own children. Ms. Holt explains why she never even considered dropping out of school: "My mother wouldn't allow it. She wasn't going [for] that drop-out stuff. Listen, she wasn't going that dropout route. There was five of us and all five of us graduated."

Ms. Holt also credits her mother for helping her to stay out of trouble when she went through a period of rebellion during early adolescence. She laughed when I asked if she got into things that she shouldn't have, "No, 'cause, my mother she wouldn't allow it. Oh God! I would have been murdered. There wouldn't be any Bradford if that was [the case]."

Some parents find fault with their own parents for not keeping on them. Ms. Horner describes a rebellious period in her younger years that she attributes to her mother's allowing her "too much freedom." She continues, "I abused it. I, I took everything for granted. Um, there was no discipline." Based on this experience, Ms. Horner believes that keeping kids on track requires a balance. She needs to be hard on her two boys but also understands that this strategy could backfire: "I am hard on my kids, I am. And um, I just hope, I just pray that um, because I'm hard on them, I don't, I try not do what my mother did [be too lenient] You know, [but] I think that it could backfire as well."

All the parents I interviewed, except for one, repeatedly spoke of the necessity of keeping children on track. The remaining parent, Ms. Green, expressed frustration with herself for not being more involved with her daughters and explained, "I could teach them how to read, but I just don't have enough, um, I just can't handle it. You know, with my condition of being [bipolar], whatever."

Ms. Green's situation may be unique, but it leads us to consider the wide range of challenges that urban families face. What is often ignored is that urban parents are attempting to support their children in school within a stressful and challenging social context (Belle, 1982); urban schools and urban communities are difficult, if not impossible, contexts to manage. Life in a poor, urban community poses challenges that can undermine the support that parents strive to give their children.

The methods by which parents raise their children and support their learning to read are grounded in their own experiences. Parents emulate their own parents yet also critique them and seek to learn from their mistakes. Parents are actively seeking ways to support their children and help them to maneuver the challenges that lie ahead.

"If Your Teacher Was Messing Around"

At our second interview, I asked Alisa, one of my first-grade students, if she ever "played school." Alisa surprised me by answering no, unlike my other first-grade students who reported playing school often at home with friends and siblings. I repeated the question, this time presenting the question hypothetically:

> *Ms. Lilly:* If you were playing school and you were the teacher what would you teach the children?
> *Alisa:* Um, he would teach the children nothing.
> *Ms. Lilly:* You wouldn't teach the children anything?
> *Alisa:* No, because if you don't, if they play they won't, they won't learn.

To Alisa the phrase *to play school* elicited a different schema from my own. Instead of thinking of the idea of "playing school," Alisa was thinking about "playing *in* school." Like the parents I interviewed, Alisa clearly believes that playing is not appropriate for school and that playing interferes with learning. Furthermore, Alisa explains that it is the teacher's responsibility to ensure that children do not play in school. Like the parents interviewed in this study, Alisa expects teachers to take an active role in helping children learn by setting limits and having high expectations. Other children I interviewed agreed; Seana explains, "If the teacher's teaching real, real lot and not playing around, you'll be the best, the best smart student in the whole world." From Alisa, Seana, and the other children in this study, I learned that my students have very clear expectations for me, their teacher.

Just as parents need to stay on their children, teachers must be firm. Mr. Sherwood points out the role that I, as the teacher, play:

> Sorry to put you on the spot today but um, teachers like you, you know, [Marvin] have a teacher that um, care, you know, and cramp down on him, you know and like um, um, Ms. Doris [Marvin's grandmother] she say, um, get on him, get on him, you know, he needs that.

The necessity of a student-teacher relationship that is both caring and demanding is perhaps best illustrated when parents compare their child's healthy teacher-children relationships with less positive relationships. Ms. Williams worked extensively with children in my class. When asked about Christy's attitude toward reading, Ms. Green responded:

> She likes it. She likes it. She likes you in particular. And this is not, I'm not saying any kind of bull job. She loves you but she doesn't like Ms. Williams because Ms. Williams yells at her. . . . She yells at everybody and she also has a, I've heard it, her attitude is the opposite of what I would use.

By yelling at the children, Ms. Williams clearly stayed on the children. However, Ms. Green does not view Ms. Williams as a caring teacher. Having high expectations for behavior must be accompanied by caring relationships that demonstrate that the teacher cares about the children.

Ms. Webster also compares Tiffany's relationship with me to Tiffany's relationship with Ms. Williams. According to Ms. Webster, "She, she loves you and she, she was learning, you know. She was learning and she enjoyed it, but then with Ms. Williams it's like she was stuck on her work." This description of Ms. Williams as being "stuck on her work" is a wonderful description of teachers who focus primarily on academic tasks without attending sufficiently to the individuals who are present. Ms. Webster contrasts a teacher's being stuck on her work with attitudes that promote loving, learning, and enjoying school. The former lacks strong personal relationships that contribute to students' learning.

Sonia Nieto records the words of Ron Morris, an African American teenager with a difficult academic history; his words describe the type of teacher Ms. Webster referred to as "stuck on her work."

> When a teacher becomes a teacher, she acts like a teacher instead of a person. She takes her title as now she's mechanical, somebody just running it. Teachers shouldn't deal with students like we're machines. You're a person. I'm a person. We come to school and we all act like people. (Nieto, 1996, p. 268)

Students also expect teachers to play an active role in helping children learn. They clearly understand that the teacher is responsible for providing appropriate learning experiences for children and are not deceived by poor teaching.

> *Lashanda:* If you have books and you couldn't read it and it was a high school book and you were 13, you couldn't read a book and your teacher was messing around and not teach you how to read you need to, you need to start all over, start all over in your life.

Jermaine also holds the teacher responsible. I asked him if there was anything else that makes reading hard. Jermaine responded, "And, and the teacher, they, she don't buy no books for them, she buy only snacks."

Like their parents, my students expect teachers to have high expectations for their students and to prevent students from playing in school. This is the teacher's responsibility and children recognize when teachers are not doing their job.

CONCLUSION

Just as Marvin's grandmother "really packed it down on him," the vast majority of parents in this study describe helping their children with reading. In this chapter, I have explored the ways in which parents support children as readers and how their roles as well as their expectations for their children's teachers are connected to their own histories. Thus parents, and subsequently their children, are the products of certain histories that encompass not only family experiences but also school experiences. The discourses that each family brings to the school are constructed within the social histories of families and their communities (Gee, 1992). These histories both align with and contradict the mainstream discourses about learning to read and urban families.

Of critical importance is the reality that some children's home and school discourses readily align, while other children encounter great disparity between the discourses (ways of using language, acting, interacting, thinking) that they use at home and those that they are expected to acquire at school.

> Some children begin schooling with analytical or strategic tools and dispositions which allow them to quickly take up the instructional ethos, culture and pedagogic routines and to focus their attention on new academic learning. (Hill et al., 1998, p. 13)

My students and their parents generally do not enjoy this advantage. As they move between home and school, they have the dual challenge of participating in an unfamiliar discourse community and confronting novel academic tasks. These challenges are compounded when educators bring negative assumptions to the classroom that deny the many resources and sources of support that children's families offer. This chapter has revealed additional mainstream discourses that surround the experience of learning to read in this urban community.

> *Urban parents don't read, can't read, and don't care about reading or their child's learning.* While the actions and the words of the parents and children presented in this chapter clearly challenge mainstream assumptions that portray urban parents as uninterested in and uncaring about learning, mainstream discourses often reverberate in the voices of parents as they describe their neighbors.

> *Urban parents do not supervise their children.* Again, while the actions and the words of parents in this study readily contradict this assumption, parents report that their neighbors do not adequately supervise their children.

> *Teachers have to be tough to teach urban children.* Parents report that they expect teachers to stay on their children. However, staying on a child is clearly differentiated from not caring or being cruel. Par-

Figure 4.1. The Home Context Situated Within Competing Discourses

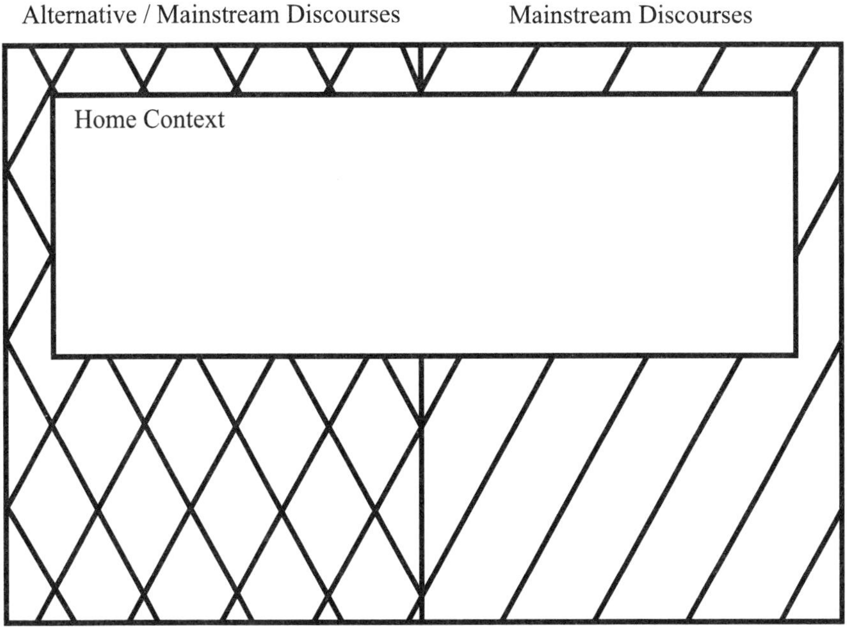

Alternative / Mainstream Discourses	Mainstream Discourses

Home Context

ents embellish this mainstream discourse about toughness with an insistence that teachers simultaneously develop supportive personal relationships with children.

A critical lesson learned from this chapter involves the ways that learning to read for a particular child is contextualized within his or her family. In the following chapter, the parents of my students describe how their own parents and even their grandparents provided resources and advice that continue to support them in helping their children learn to read.

Figure 4.1 captures how experiences related to learning to read are contextualized within the families of my students. Beliefs, attitudes, and practices of children's parents, grandparents, and even great grandparents continue to contribute to my students' experiences with reading. These family dimensions are generally denied or ignored as urban families are routinely portrayed as deficit and incompetent.

It must be remembered that the home experiences that surround the process of learning to read function within larger social, economic, and political contexts that reflect both mainstream and alternative discourses.

Thus, in this contextualized model of reading, the home context is super-imposed upon Figure 3.2 to demonstrate how the experiences of families are always subject to both mainstream and alternative discourses operating within historical, economic, and social contexts.

In the following chapter, I will further explore the role that family members play in helping children learn how to read while also examining additional relationships that surround the experience of learning to read for my students.

5

The Role of Social Relationships in Learning to Read

One morning, six students and I gathered on the rug in the front of my classroom with our books. As the children assembled, I asked them a routine question that I hoped would stimulate their thinking about my intended focus for our reading lesson that day.

> *Ms. Lilly:* Why did I put you together in a group? Leshanda?
> *Leshanda:* Help people.
> *Ms. Lilly:* Sometimes you help people. But why did, the main reason I put you together? Jasmine?
> *Jasmine:* So that we can read together.
> *Ms. Lilly:* Yeah, but why did I want you guys to read together? Alisa?
> *Alisa:* Cuz we could be friends.
> *Ms. Lilly:* Yeah. James?
> *James:* Listen [to the teacher].
> *Ms. Lilly:* These are things that I want you to do.
> *Jasmine:* Help, help people when they get stuck on a word.
> *Ms. Lilly:* What is it? Yeah you guys do all those good things but what is it that you guys don't do sometimes when you read that I want you to be more careful about? What is it? Alisa?
> *Alisa:* The words.
> *Ms. Lilly:* Hmmm, you don't know all the words do you? Hmmm, what do you do when you make a mistake?
> *Leshanda:* Go back and try it again.

Finally, I elicit the response I was seeking. Despite my attempts to focus on a reading strategy, the children were focused on one another and the social relationships they share. It was not until I clearly directed them to attend to my agenda that the desired response was elicited. The children in my class are clearly aware of the social context that accompanies learning to read. While I was promoting my instructional agenda and focusing on helping students to improve their reading processes, my students were focused on the individuals around them and the relationships they have with their peers.

In the previous chapter, I explored the role parents play in helping children learn to read. In this chapter I will address additional social relationships that surround the experience of learning to read for my students. My research reveals that parents and children are highly cognizant of the social relationships that surround learning to read; this research reminds educators of the need to recognize and respect these personal relationships as well as personal histories of individuals and families.

My introduction to the reading lesson described earlier reflects mainstream discourses about learning to read. According to these discourses, learning to read is assumed to be a solitary process in which children practice and master specific skills and strategies necessary for decoding and comprehending texts. Within this discourse, teachers, like myself, tend to neglect the social and collaborative aspects of reading while focusing on individual demonstration of skill and strategies (for example, rereading challenging sections of text).

In urban schools, this tendency is exaggerated by the negative assumptions educators often make about their students and their families. Too often schools have created spaces where parents are not welcome. According to Madeline Grumet, one component of becoming a teacher involves learning discourses that denigrate parents. She insists that teachers and parents must "make peace" (1988, p. 178) and acknowledge a solidarity based on their shared interest in children. Rather than accepting mainstream discourses that degrade and criticize urban families, educators must establish healthy relationships with families that can lead educators to challenge mainstream assumptions about these families.

Many researchers have addressed the importance of social relationships in schools (Dyson, 1993; Grumet, 1988; Kohl, 1994; Ladson-Billings, 1994; Madigan & Koivu-Rybicki, 1997). Nel Noddings maintains that students must be engaged in caring relationships as "the very bedrock of all successful education" (1992, p. 27). Noddings laments that children and especially adolescents often feel that people in schools do not care about them or their education.

Social relationships are significant factors in learning to read. David Bloome explains:

> The social relationships involved in reading include establishing social groups and ways of interacting with others; gaining or maintaining

status and social position; and acquiring culturally appropriate ways of thinking, problem solving, valuing and feeling. (1985, p. 134)

However, these relationships are not always recognized and nurtured in schools. Noddings (1992) describes the ways teachers devalue personal relationships and tend to focus on instructional objectives:

The idea is to make the individual teacher, the individual student, and their relations irrelevant to the success of instruction which is posited as the primary goal of schooling. Once objectives are chosen, teachers are not supposed to deviate from them. They are to seek means within a narrowly defined standard form to reach the objectives, and further, the objectives now established are almost entirely cognitive. The purposes and objectives of the student are ignored (indeed denied as random behavior) unless they happen to coincide with those of the teacher. (p. 10)

Educational objectives take center stage; relationships are assumed to be irrelevant, as are the purposes and objectives of students. In this chapter I will further examine the social relationships that surround the process of learning to read.

RELATIONSHIPS IN AN URBAN COMMUNITY

Relationships that participants describe in terms of learning to read extend beyond the classroom door. James Wertsch (1990) argues that in order to understand human behavior we must reconstruct all the points in the development of that behavior; activities that families engage in to help children learn to read are chronologically contextualized within family and community histories. Denny Taylor agrees; she describes her reaction to the middle-class parents she interviewed about reading: "I was continuously impressed by the way parents' interpretations of the present were bound by their recollections of the past" (1983, p. 22).

Parent and student perspectives will be presented to explore the roles parents and grandparents, teachers, peers, and siblings play in supporting children as they learn to read. These relationships will be looked at in terms of how they contribute to children's experiences with learning to read. Examination of the social relationships that accompany reading reveals not only the manner in which these relationships are defined by mainstream discourses, but also how these relationships are experienced within families as they support children in learning to read. In this chapter, the respective roles of teachers and mothers will be explored along with the roles of other family members, teachers, peers, and siblings.

"I Guess It's Both of Us"

As the teacher of the children in this study, I avoided asking parents directly about their relationship with me. I feared that parents would answer politely and avoid making comments that they thought I would not appreciate. One question that I did ask was "Whose responsibility is it to teach children how to read?"

Some parents indicated that especially during the early years, parents have the primary responsibility for helping children. Ms. Rodriguez was adamant that parents were responsible for teaching their children "the basics" of reading. For Ms. Rodriguez, the basics include teaching children their ABC's, some words, and reading aloud to children; she reports that it was her mother who taught her how to read.

Six out of the nine parents who were asked reported that parents and teachers share responsibility for helping children learn to read. Five of these parents indicated that the parents' role is primary, especially in the early years. Ms. Horner describes how she prepared Peter for school; she speaks with affection about Peter's great-grandmother:

> My grandmother told me [laughs], she told me when uh, Peter was a little baby, she says, "You say the ABC's to him and you count to him, 1 to 20, every single day and maybe even a couple of times a day so that as he gets older he will be up a little, you know. Uh, he'll be familiar with, um the letters and the numbers.". . . So that's what I did with him and at a young age he would, he was able to count, he could say his ABC's so he was there and that's one, one thing that Mr. Tonkin said about him in kindergarten. Like that, Peter knew so much coming in already. I love that.

Ms. Horner takes us back four generations, describing how her grandmother advised her to work with her son on letters and numbers. Ms. Horner attributes Peter's success in kindergarten to this advice. Peter's success is a great source of pride to his mother.

Ms. Holt describes the primary role of the parent and the ongoing interaction between teacher and parent in supporting the student.

> Learning starts at home. I figure if I get them going and the teacher helps me out we'll be helping my child. Because she [the teacher] goes to school to know how to do it the right way. I can try too, if she, if she gets him going I can keep him going because I didn't go to college to teach him the right way. I can teach him

what I know which may be wrong with the finger movement or whatever, but they may not want to use that finger movement in school.

Ms. Holt agrees that learning starts at home. She believes that she has a role in helping her children get ready for school. However, she explains that the teacher will "know how to do it the right way." Ms. Holt acknowledges the teacher's special training and worries that she might teach Bradford in the wrong way. She believes that teachers have expertise and skills that she does not. Ms. Holt accepts mainstream discourses that define the teacher as the expert while calling into question the skills and abilities of parents.

Ms. Webster disagrees; while she does help Tiffany, she believes that teaching Tiffany to read is primarily the school's responsibility. She makes an interesting distinction: "I help her, but you're [referring to me, the teacher-researcher] teaching her how to read." However, Ms. Webster indicates that this is a point of contention between her and her boyfriend.

> Ms. Webster: Well, Reginald says it's me [who should be teaching Tiffany to read].
> Ms. Lilly: That's your boyfriend?
> Ms. Webster: Yeah, he says it's my responsibility cuz I had her. But I think it, well it's actually me but it's the school too. Because that's what the school's there for. I told him a minute ago, I said well if the school ain't going to teach her then she might as well stay home and I'll teach her how. You know?
> Ms. Lilly: Home schooling, right?
> Ms. Webster: Yeah, I said, well, why's she going up there and he's like, no that's not the point. You know, you had her and you're supposed to be teaching her too. I guess, I guess it's both of us.

Interestingly, Ms. Webster is the only parent interviewed who reported that she did not learn to read from her mother. Her own experience as the youngest of 10 children in a struggling rural family may have demonstrated to her the role that schools can play in helping children learn to read. Throughout this conversation, Ms. Webster's words are offered hesitantly with a constant shift between positions. She suggests that helping Tiffany learn to read is the teachers responsibility but then agrees that it's her responsibility as well. She then questions the purpose of the school if it isn't to teach children how to read, but then resolves the issue by saying that it is both of their responsibilities. While mainstream discourses would suggest that urban students learn to read in school, Ms. Webster adopts this discourse and then challenges it, citing the possibility of a dual responsibility between home and school.

Mr. Sherwood reports a similar disagreement between him and his wife:

> I had a little problem with her [Marvin's grandmother] upstairs. . . . They [parental figures, including Marvin's grandmother] figure, ask them, they [children] leave the house [for school], you're [motioning to me, the teacher] responsible for them not me. . . . I dress them, I dress him for school or they dress theirselves, they, it's out of my hands. Which is wrong. You know, they out of my hands, and that's, that's the way they feel.

Mr. Sherwood clearly disagrees with his wife; he indicates that it is wrong for parents to believe that once children are sent to school that it is just the teacher's responsibility. He explains that Marvin's grandmother, along with other parents, describe themselves as being responsible for getting children off to school and then it is "out of my hands." Interestingly, despite her adamance that teaching children to read is the teachers' responsibility, Marvin's grandmother spends significant amounts of time helping Marvin.

In contrast, Ms. Green recognizes her responsibility to help Christy learn to read but attributes her inability to help Christy to her long history of mental illness, which she refers to here as "my condition." She laughs uncomfortably and explains:

> Well, I don't know, with me, uh, I could teach them how to read. But I don't have enough, um, I just can't handle it. You know with my condition of being whatever . . . I swear to God, I barely read to them. It's I, I can read cuz um, I can read really well, but I just can't do it. I just can't, something about a mental state, I mean that I have. I, I just can't do it. So if you all don't teach them to read they gonna . . . [voice trails off].

Ms. Green recognizes her role in helping Christy learn to read; she also recognizes that she is academically and intellectually capable of fulfilling this task. However, she leaves the responsibility for teaching children to read to the teachers. As she explains, she just can't manage it due to her "mental state." Although she does not complete her thought, it is clear that there will be negative consequences for Christy if "you all [the teachers] don't do it [teach Christy to read]."

Despite points of contention and difficulty, most parents in this study view the parents and teachers as having complementary and collaborative roles in helping children learn to read. While mainstream discourses about urban parents question the ability and initiative of urban parents to help their children with learning to read, the parents interviewed for this study believe that they play a critical role in helping their children learn to read. In contrast to mainstream discourses that portray parents as uninterested, uncaring, lazy, or lacking the academic skills required to support their children, the parents in this study both recognize their responsibility and work to support their children.

"My Whole Family"

When I asked my students who helps them with their reading, my students generally mentioned their mothers first.

> *Ms. Lilly:* Who's helping you learn to read?
> *Jermaine:* My mom.
> *Ms. Lilly:* Anyone else?
> *Jermaine:* And my teacher.

However, students consistently mentioned many other people in addition to mothers and teachers who help them with their reading. When asked who helped him learn to read, Javon and his peers offer long lists of family members.

> *Javon:* My mom, my uncle, my aunt, my grandma and my mom's sister, Mary, Lavon, Nico, Justin, and Kevin.

> *Jasmine:* My mother, my father, my grandmother, my aunt, and my other aunt, and my cousin.

> *Alisa:* My mommy, my daddy, my whole family.

Children in this study recognize many people as resources in the process of learning to read. Javon's, Jasmine's, and Alisa's lists include mothers, fathers, older brothers and sisters, a twin brother, cousins, aunts, and grandmothers. Older siblings are never left off my students' lists.

"If It Wasn't for Her"

Children report seeking assistance from a variety of sources and finding many people willing and able to help them with learning to read. However, most children identified their mother (or in Marvin's case his grandmother) as the primary person who helps them with reading. Six of the 10 students also report that their fathers or father figures are helping them learn to read, although fathers appear to be less involved than mothers. Four households do not have a male adult in the home; however, some of the students whose fathers do not live with them are among the students who report that their fathers help them with their reading.

David reports that his father helps him with his reading, although his mother reports that his father can read and write very little. Jermaine and his mother agree that although Jermaine's father can read very well, he does not help Jermaine with his reading. Mr. Sherwood reports doing many things to help Marvin learn to read; however, he reports that Marvin's grandmother does much more.

While children list many people who help them with their reading, consistent with mainstream expectations, mothers in this community, rather than fathers, are primarily responsible for helping children learn to read. Even Christy reports that her mother helps her learn to read, despite her mother's assertions to the contrary.

Parents also believe that their own mothers were active in helping them learn to read. The voices of parents are full of pride as they speak of their mothers.

Ms. Hudson: With my mother, we did a lot of reading.

Ms. Johnson: She [her mother] used to sit, you know, and take time with me and read books with me and stories and everything. Way back when I can't remember. You know, a little kid.

Ms. Horner: I know my mom always bought me books and that was a definite. Uh, I've always been surrounded by books. I've always had a big bookshelf, uh, she bought me encyclopedias so that when we had reports to do in school and all that all my information was just right there.

Mr. Sherwood: If it weren't for her [his mother], and her, cuz its just us anyways, I wouldn't be able to read. I like that.

The primary role of mothers was evident when parents were asked who taught them to read. Seven out of nine parents reported at some point during the interviews that their mothers taught them how to read. Another parent reports that she taught herself to read with help from her older brothers and sisters. Only one parent gave primary credit to the school.

Ms. Webster reports that the teacher she had when she repeated first grade taught her to read; she speaks of this teacher with great affection. However, Ms. Webster also mentions an older sister who read with her at home.

Mr. Sherwood describes how his mother taught him to read when learning to read at school proved challenging:

> They just give us the book. "What is this?" . . . Uh I probably said "the," "sit," or "Dick and Jane," you know, I was just mumbling through the whole thing. That's when I think I told my mother about it . . . and she said it's time for you to get a library card . . . . Every Saturday morning, we had to go to the library and we stayed at the library until we picked up on our reading.

The idea that participants' mothers taught them to read contradicts mainstream discourses about schools and particularly about primary classrooms. Certainly, the first-grade curriculum reflects the assumption that children learn to read in school. First-grade teachers, including myself, often claim a sense of efficacy and pride based on the belief that we teach children to read. The words of parents captured here challenge educators to consider the possibility that learning to read occurs in multiple contexts and that the parental role may be much greater than assumed, particularly in urban communities.

"You Learn Fast That Way"

While parents credit their mothers with having the greatest impact on their learning to read, they also tell stories about their own teachers. Some parents describe teachers who went beyond the required textbook to make reading more interesting. Ms. Rodriguez explains, "We had a lot of plays and a lot of poems that we used to read and that was interesting to me. The regular textbook wasn't interesting. It was like I'm going to sleep. I can't read that." Ms. Rodriguez contrasts using the "regular textbook" with using plays and poems to teach. For Ms. Rodriguez, reading the textbook led to "going to sleep" while plays and poems were interesting to her.

Ms. Johnson also describes good teachers as making learning fun. "You know [he'd play] word games and stuff with you and it made it easier to learn. You wanted to learn it." Ms. Webster describes a teacher with a similar approach:

> Every time she would get ready to teach us something she would put like a game to it and that's how we learned is like through the

games and stuff. It was a lot of fun and you learn fast that way. She got us really, we did really good.

Ms. Webster explains that games and fun help children to learn faster and contribute to their doing well in school.

Ms. Johnson recalls her kindergarten teacher taking extra time with her after school, "We used to sit there and we'd pick out books and she'd sit there and we'd read together. I'd stay there after school and do that with her. . . . I loved it. She was my favorite teacher throughout school." This teacher recognized the power of close personal relationships.

Based on the stories parents tell as described in this and the preceding chapter, parents clearly value teachers who make learning interesting yet are both caring and tough with their students. Strong personal relationships are critical to students and their parents. By making reading exciting and insisting that children learn, teachers demonstrate to students that they care.

"They Let You Learn"

Despite the primary role of mothers, 8 out of 10 students also credited their teachers with helping them learn to read. To my young students, the actions and activities of the teacher are almost magical. Students describe what teachers do as if their actions easily and automatically result in children learning to read. Students report teachers doing a variety of things to help children learn to read:

> *Javon:* They, they [teachers] let them go get their own book and I read.
> *Peter:* She [the teacher] made us read a lo—, a lot. She read stories to us. That's all.
> *Javon:* They um, they let you learn.
> *Ms. Lilly:* Is there anything else they do? [Pause] What else do teachers do?
> *Javon:* They um, they decide if you going to second [grade] or not.
> *Marvin:* [The teachers] get books for the kids to read it.
> *Peter:* They um, the teachers help them and they have to pay attention. That's how they [children] learn to read.
> *Ms. Lilly:* Anything else they have to do?
> *Peter:* They have to do their tests.

Students report many ways teachers transform children into readers. For Javon it appears to be important that teachers simply let them get books and let the child learn. Peter explains that all I did was make them read a lot and read stories to them. He later explains that the children have responsibilities too; they need to pay attention and do their tests. Marvin believes that teachers help children learn to read by getting the books for children. In each of these descriptions, the teacher does something very simple (get the books, read the stories, lets the children learn, makes them read) and reading simply ensues. To the children, the teachers' role appears minimal, practically effortless, and remarkably effective.

On a very few occasions students refer to specific classroom activities. Jermaine sensed that the procedures used in guided reading groups contribute to his learning to read. He explained what the teacher does:

> Um they take them to the floor. Every day and they be read[ing]. They read the same books [familiar books] and a hard, a other [new book]. [The reading group is] where you get a hard book.

Jermaine attributes his learning to his taking part in these procedures. Peter alludes specifically to the skills teachers teach:

Peter: Some of their teachers help them to use the sounds.
Ms. Lilly: Uh-huh. What do teachers do to help them?
Peter: They have the pictures of words like *X* and *C*. They make them do the sounds. They teach them.

Peter seems to believe that teachers "make" children practice things that help them learn to read. He explains that teachers "make them do the sounds," while earlier he explains that I "made" them read a lot. Peter seems to understand the teacher's role as making children do what is necessary so that learning will occur. While precisely what teachers do is explained only on rare occasions, students do believe that their teachers help them learn to read.

"Maybe Their Friends Taught Them"

My students also mention the role their peers play in helping them learn to read.

Ms. Lilly: Who's helping you to learn [to read]?
Bradford: Marvin.
Ms. Lilly: Marvin. Anyone else?
Bradford: Devin.
Ms. Lilly: Mmm-hmm, who else?
Bradford: David.

Interestingly, Bradford mentioned his two best friends as the people helping him to learn to read.

Some students even credited the teacher in the class next door with
helping them learn to read although she never taught my students. Marvin
explained how Mr. Matthews, the school principal, helps children learn
to read: "[He] send[s] you to school and tells the teachers to make the
kids be [good] so they can go into second grade and they can go to
college."

The idea that children can help one another with reading recurs
throughout the interviews. When asked what they would like to be better
at when they read, both Peter and Javon reply that they would like to
help the other children. Javon explains that he would like to help by
"working on hard words that people don't know and then I could ask
the teacher can I tell them what the hard words are." Helping other
children to read has both personal and social value. Personally, children
are likely to feel good about themselves when they are able to read words
that their peers cannot. Socially, children are likely to gain academic status
in a classroom when they are able to support others.

Children in this class view their peers as capable of helping one
another. When asked who helped him learn to read, Marvin listed his
best friends: Bradford, Devin, and David. In a discussion about who might
have taught their parents to read, Peter suggests that "maybe their friends
taught them how to read." Peter's friends at day care help him:

> *Ms. Lilly:* Oh, how are your friends at day care helping you?
>   That's interesting.
> *Peter:* Sometimes when I have homework, when I don't know
>   what the word says, they help me out.
> *Ms. Lilly:* Are they grownup friends or kid friends?
> *Peter:* Kid friends.
> *Ms. Lilly:* Oh, are they older than you?
> *Peter:* Yes.

In the following example, Jerome and Bradford, two struggling readers, demonstrate an amazing degree of reciprocal support and interaction
as they collaboratively read a version of Aesop's "The Lion and the
Mouse" from our basal reader:

> *Ms. Lilly:* What did he do? He, rrr . . .
> [Once the boys are started, Ms. Lilly moves on to work with other
>   students and leaves the audiotape recording]
> *Bradford:* . . . ran up the lion.

Jerome: He ran down the lion.
Bradford: He ran down the lion. Man, you ain't even reading.
Jerome: Yes, I'm is.
Bradford and Jerome: Stop said the lion. Your play time is over mouse now I will eat you. The mouse said—
Jerome: No.
Bradford: Let—
Jerome: Look—
Bradford: Let, let . . .
Bradford and Jerome: [Jerome echoing] . . . me go. [Together] The lion said I could say yes I could say no. Lions have . . .
Bradford: . . . to go.
Bradford and Jerome: Lions have the say and I say no.
[This interaction continues for another 35 exchanges]

Although both struggling readers, Bradford and Jerome are able to work together to read this challenging text. These students independently support each other and maintain meaningful interaction with the text. Bradford and Jerome are close friends; their friendship is central to this reading experience. Individually, these students would have easily become frustrated with reading this text and may not have been able to maintain interest.

At least once during the interview process children were asked who in their class they felt was a good reader. Figure 5.1 presents the children's responses. Seven different children were identified by their peers as good readers. Of these seven only two of the children identified by their peers are among the best readers in the class according to my assessments (running records and story retellings).

Peter and Diamond were among the highest-performing readers in the class. Diamond was in the highest reading group throughout the entire year. Peter moved into this group in mid-October. Both children were reading and comprehending easily at the second-grade level by February. Both Peter and Diamond were generally helpful to their peers and readily agreed to work with children who did not read as well as they did. When I interviewed his peers, Peter was identified four times as a good reader; Diamond was identified twice. Interestingly, the strongest reader in the class, James, was not identified by any of his peers. James often chose to read alone and was generally not part of social interactions that occurred around books. While he was an excellent reader, James was less in demand as a reading partner than either Peter or Diamond.

Marvin, Leshanda, and Lecara moved between the two middle reading groups. They made average progress. All three were personable chil-

Figure 5.1. Teacher Assessment of Children and
the Number of Times Children Were
Recognized by Peers as Good Readers

Teacher Assessment	Times Children Were Identified
HIGH-ACHIEVING STUDENTS	
Peter	4
Diamond	2
MIDDLE-ACHIEVING STUDENTS	
Marvin	3
Leshanda	3
Lecara	2
LOW-ACHIEVING STUDENTS	
Nadine	3
Jermaine	1

dren and were often sought as reading partners by their peers. These
children were identified as good readers by two or three of their peers
during the interviews.

Although Jermaine and Nadine finished the year near the middle of
the class in terms of their reading achievement, they began as two of the
lowest-performing children in the class. Both children spent many weeks
in Reading Recovery to address their difficulties with reading. Neither
Jermaine nor Nadine were among the strongest readers in the class based
on teacher assessments.

Children in this study often identified a close friend as being a good
reader (Figure 5.2). Two children identified their best friends as good
readers. Bradford consistently selected Marvin; while Christy selected
Nadine. In Christy's case, she is a much stronger reader than Nadine.
Generally, my students identified children whom they found to be good
reading partners as good readers. For example, Peter reports that Leshanda is a good reader "cuz she's nice." Likewise, Alisa explains that
Lecara is a good reader because "Lecara is nice and she be nice to everyone
in the classroom." Javon also identifies Lecara as a good reader. His older
sister teases him; she knows that Javon has a crush on Lecara. Certainly
a good reader does more than read words correctly. By identifying a good
reader as someone who is good to read with, children recognize reading as

Figure 5.2. Who Was Identified by Whom as a Good Reader

Child Interviewed	Child Identified	Teacher Assessment	Comments
Christy	Nadine	low	best friends
	Nadine	low	best friends
Jasmine	Lecara	middle/high	says that Diamond is "*really* good"
Diamond	Peter	high	
Peter	Leshanda	middle	"cuz she's nice"
	Leshanda	middle	
Jermaine	Peter	high	
	Nadine	low	
Marvin	Leshanda	middle	
	Jermaine	low	
Bradford	Marvin	middle	best friends
	Marvin	middle	best friends
Javon	Lecara	middle	has a "crush" on Lecara
	Peter	high	
Alisa	Diamond	high	"she be nice to everyone"
	Lecara	middle	
David	Peter	high	
	Marvin	middle	
Tiffany	Alisa	middle	

inseparable from the social context and the relationships that accompany learning to read in school.

The ways my students describe their peers as readers contributes to an understanding of reading as a socially constructed concept. When students judge their peers as good readers based on criteria that include who is good to read with, one must ask if children apply these same criteria to themselves. Are they good readers because other children choose to read with them? What does it mean when other children choose not read with them?

"They Got Brothers for That"

In addition to peers, children and parents describe the important role that siblings play in learning to read. Alisa explains how her older brothers read with her. Ms. Rodriguez confirms this; she explains that she doesn't have to read to Alisa and her little sister, because "they got brothers for that. They brothers read to them."

When identifying the people who help them learn to read, parents' and children's lists often include siblings. Ms. Holt explains that Bradford's teenage sister is more successful in helping Bradford than she is. Bradford's mother adjusts her voice to re-create the dialogue:

> His older sister helps him when he gets his homework. I sit there [saying] "Bradford, that's not right." [Bradford's sister replies] "Mommy?" [Ms. Holt continues] "Bradford, that's not right." [Bradford's sister steps in] "Mommy, I'll help him." She give it [help]. Before you know it it's almost done [Ms. Holt laughs]. . . . But she's still in school so they know the rules, the tricks and how it's done.

Ms. Holt performs this scene revealing how she becomes frustrated with helping Bradford with his homework. As she re-creates this dialogue, the re-created voice of Bradford's sister brings a calming feeling to the scene. At 44 years old, Ms. Bradford has been out of school for a long time. She talked often in our interviews about how educational practices have changed and how teachers know how to do things the "right way." By re-creating this dialogue, Ms. Bradford demonstrates to me how despite her own feelings of inadequacy and frustration, Bradford has the support he needs at home to complete his homework. As she explains, his sister is "still in school" and knows how things are done.

Ms. Horner is counting on Peter to help his little brother when he goes to school.

> *Ms. Horner:* My youngest is starting kindergarten this year and, and I'm like, oh my gosh, please.
> *Ms. Lilly:* Oh, he'll be fine.
> *Ms. Horner:* Please, please, I know Peter. He's going to work with him [his little brother] though.

While Ms. Horner sounded a bit anxious about her younger son starting kindergarten, she is comforted by the fact that she knows that Peter is going to help the younger one.

Ms. Webster describes how her older sister helped her learn to read. The youngest in a family of 10 children, Ms. Webster explains that her mother worked a lot and couldn't help her with academic tasks.

> My sister used to read to me. I used to beg her and she used to read to me, but, bedtime stories. She used to hate doing it too . . . . I used to beg her and she'd read to me at night. But not all the time, not all the time. There was not very much reading done in our house. Not much going on.

Both students and parents recognize the role siblings play in helping children learn to read. Parents view older siblings as resources that they can tap to support younger children as they learn to read.

CONCLUSION

The relationships that surround reading often appear contradictory. Mothers accept their role as their child's first teachers, yet report that teachers, unlike parents, know the right way to do it. Parents believe that their mothers taught them to read, whereas mainstream discourses would credit teachers; however, students describe teachers as simply "let[ting] you learn" or "read[ing] stories to us" and thus learning to read magically occurs. These apparent contradictions constantly arise in conversations about reading and contribute to the complexity of understanding reading relationships.

Reading relationships reflect wide ranges of experiences that occur across lifetimes and over generations. In most schools, however, relationships between participants are treated as secondary to the instructional objectives of the classroom. As Ms. Webster reported in Chapter Four, too often the teacher is "stuck on her work." In this chapter I have introduced and challenged additional mainstream discourses about reading.

> *Learning to read is a process of learning new skills.* While parents and children in this study tend to ascribe to mainstream discourses that conceptualize reading as a process of decoding text (sounding out words and identifying words), parents and children also recognize the importance of the social relationships that surround learning to read.

> *Teachers teach children how to read.* While most parents recognized a joint responsibility between teachers and parents in helping chil-

dren learn to read, with one exception, parents describe their own mothers as teaching them how to read. Mainstream discourses that label urban parents as illiterate and uninterested are clearly challenged by parents and children in this study who identified their own mothers as central in their process of learning to read.

Being a good reader entails reading accurately, with fluency and comprehension. Students in this study describe being a good reader as being a person who is good to read with rather than one who has simply mastered the technical skills of reading.

In this chapter, parents, teachers, siblings, and peers are all identified as helping children learn to read. Brian Street uses the term "literacy practices" to refer to "both behavior and the social and cultural conceptualizations that give meaning to the uses of reading and writing" (1995, p. 2). For the children in my class, learning to read is not just a matter of the skills and strategies I teach them in the classroom. Learning to read involves a rich array of activities and a vast cast of characters who contribute extensively to my students' experiences with reading. As is demonstrated in this chapter, learning to read involves home and school as well as the past experiences and insights of many people.

While Figure 4.1 presented the role of home experiences in learning to read, Figure 5.3 presents what the school brings to the process of learning to read. In the lower portion of the diagram, the role of teachers and peers is presented. When home and school contexts are superimposed on Figure 3.2 (see Figure 5.3), one half of each figure falls upon mainstream discourses, while the other half falls upon alternative discourses. What we have created is a complex social field in which students, parents, and teachers function. Some participants will participate primarily in mainstream discourse communities that fall to the right side of the diagram; these people tend to ascribe to mainstream discourses about reading and/or about the communities in which they teach. Based on their relative lack of lived experiences that contradict mainstream ideologies (Fairclough, 1989), White, middle-class teachers may tend to be situated to the right. Other participants may routinely access alternative discourses to understand their world. These participants will experience the tensions that accompany alternative ways of viewing the world and will be situated to the left side of this diagram. Urban parents, whose life experiences have often contradicted mainstream ways of understanding the world, may often fall to the left of this contextualized model of reading.

This model is clearly inadequate in capturing the complex dimensions of people acting within ideologically laden social contexts. Participation

Figure 5.3. The Home and School Contexts Situated Within Competing
Discourses

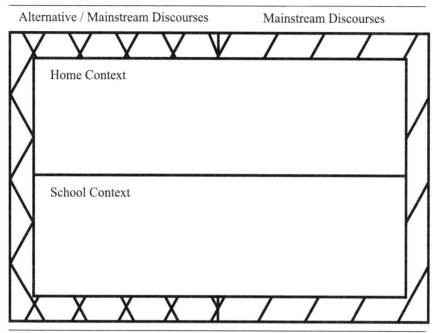

Alternative / Mainstream Discourses   Mainstream Discourses

Home Context

School Context

in discourse communities is always emerging, changing, and adapting to fluctuating social contexts; locating the exact position of a person's positioning within a discourse community is impossible because of this continual shifting. However, in a broad, awkward, and generalizing manner, this diagram begins to capture the differences that often separate urban teachers from the families of their students. While teachers often function within the contexts of mainstream discourses in terms of the ways they speak, act, and interact and in their beliefs, the parents of their students have often found those mainstream discourses to be flawed, questionable, debilitating, and successful in deflecting attention away from critical problems faced by people in urban communities.

6

The Construction of
Urban Reading Identities

One of my student's parents, Ms. Webster, referred to people who read a lot as "bookworms" and "bookish people" who "don't have no fun." She explained, "All they do is sit in the house and read books all day long or sit outside and read books."

I was surprised to hear Ms. Webster describe avid readers so negatively. In fact, during this same interview Ms. Webster describes herself as enjoying reading; however, she clearly separates herself from bookworms. Interestingly, Ms. Webster's description is typical of how the parents of my students distance themselves from "real" readers despite their own accounts of themselves as competent, enthusiastic readers.

The stories my students' parents tell reveal how their views of themselves as readers are caught up in their life experiences and their understandings of the world. Within this dynamic, there are "cultural models" or "pictures of prototypical worlds in which prototypical events occur" (Gee, 1990, p. 87). Cultural models related to reading are generally accepted understandings about readers and reading within a local community. These cultural models play a role in the development of reading identities as people define themselves as readers in reference to shared conceptions of reading and readers. For example, there are prototypical models of good readers that people within local communities may individually or collectively reject or accept. Prototypical depictions of reading and readers may contradict or support cultural practices within local communities.

While describing literacy as a valued skill in American society, Kathleen McCormick (1994) recognizes a cultural suspicion directed at people who enjoy reading. The average American is portrayed as more likely to watch TV or "surf the Net" for information than read a newspaper or book. Reading is often viewed as an intellectual, solitary activity. From Ichabod Crane to Diane Chambers (from the sitcom *Cheers*), those who read a lot are depicted as strange and socially estranged.

This suspicion may be particularly strong in urban communities where life experiences have demonstrated to residents that reading is identified with people other than themselves. Negative school experiences and low-level employment opportunities distinguish urban residents from people they perceive to be "real" readers. Furthermore, being a real reader is perceived to entail adopting attitudes and behaviors that can collide with local cultural practices and values.

PARENTS' READING IDENTITIES

In this chapter I will explore the reading identities of the parents of my students; their identities will be examined in terms of their views of themselves as readers, their past experiences with reading, and the importance of the relationship between the teacher and the child. The stories parents tell about reading reveal facets of their identities and how they position themselves relative to reading (Lieblich, Turval-Mashiach, & Zibler, 1998). The interviews also reveal the ways parents' reading identities are contextualized within their lives and their understandings about the world. In this section, I will present stories from parents that revolve around three themes. The first set of stories explore the ways parents view themselves as readers. The second set presents stories that explore parents' school reading experiences and how these experiences may have contributed to the ways they view themselves as readers. The final set of stories returns to the theme of relationships to examine how relationships between teachers and students intersect with parents' reading identities.

"But I Like to Read"

Although all the parents in the sample describe themselves as competent readers who are able to read materials necessary for functioning in their daily lives, most parents did not define themselves as that "certain" type of people who are real readers. In fact, the parents of my students describe people who are real readers as different from themselves. Ms. Horner associated real readers with "professional people" "like doctors, lawyers, definitely teachers." Other parents explain that these people "look at the world with different eyes," were a certain "type of child," constantly carried a book and pad for writing, were "smart," and "want to know everything."
Ms. Green seemed to know these types of people well:

> *Ms. Green:* But see there's the type of people, you know the type
> they go, they never stop thirsting for knowledge and want to

know everything and anything. They never stop and I don't know what you call 'em. That's what they [Ms. Green's parents] were.

Ms. Lilly: That's what your parents were?

Ms. Green: Yeah. They would listen to the classical music station and all this stuff. Watch PBS. Watch that what-cha-ma-call-it McNeil Lehrer stuff on TV, still. My mother watched the whole contra stuff on TV every day. All that. Vietnam stuff too. I mean they had *Time* in there, *Newsweek,* they had the *New York Times.* But they did teach me one thing. I do not think that you necessarily have to stop learning. You learn at every age. School stuff.

Ms. Green describes her parents as "real" readers and notes their never-ending search for knowledge. Consistent with the view of reading as a cultural practice, Ms. Green associates being a real reader with more than reading behaviors; being a reader encompasses a range of activities and attitudes several of which do not actually involve reading. Activities such as watching PBS, the McNeil Lehrer news show, the Iran-contra trials, or coverage of Vietnam are cited as evidence of being real readers. To Ms. Green a real reader is certain "type" of person who listens to classical music and subscribes to *Newsweek* and the *New York Times.* Being a real reader entails behaviors and attitudes that extend beyond reading practices.

Mr. Sherwood identifies real readers as "loners" who don't want to be bothered with things other than their books:

As a matter of fact um, I, I got a guy at work that's all he do. He go [Mr. Sherwood picks up a newspaper off a nearby table and hides his face behind it] and he reads. That's, you know what? Let me tell you, he can um, he can like to talk about strange things. I'm serious, I'm talking about science fiction and you know this and this going to happen and you know and very smart cuz he, cuz he reads. . . . You know when person's a loner they all read. All loners read. But he don't want to be bothered with [anything] except this stuff right here. [Mr. Sherwood points to the paper again as he speaks the last sentence, indicating that the text is the reader's only interest].

While Mr. Sherwood expresses a certain appreciation for his friend who reads a lot, when he explains that his friend is "very smart cuz he reads," there is also a sense that too much reading isolates people from their peers. This "guy" doesn't want to be bothered by other things besides reading. Mr. Sherwood's friend is described as a loner for whom reading has replaced both social relationships and the real world. Mr. Sherwood goes on to describe the "strange" things his friend talks about. Just as Ms. Green describes being a real reader as encompassing more than reading behaviors, Mr. Sherwood associates being a real reader with being antisocial and strange.

Ms. Webster provides a thought-provoking example of the way reading may be viewed as antisocial. Ms. Webster describes how her boyfriend discourages her from reading:

> *Ms. Webster:* Kids, job, cleaning, boyfriend. If I had a day, just a day all to myself, I mean and get me some books, I could read all them books in one day but it's like you got so many interruptions. [Imitating her daughter] "Maaa"; [imitating her boyfriend] "Karen, what are you doing? Come sit with me." You know it, it's like if I'm sitting here in the night and I be reading, he'll flip the light off on me. He'll turn the light off.
> *Ms. Lilly:* Just to get your attention?
> *Ms. Webster:* Just to say quit reading, OK? You're supposed to spend time with me and not read books. That's what he does. Cuz he, he says to me more than one time, put the light off. And I'll go in the kitchen or in the bedroom and read.

Ms. Webster explains that the demands of daily life and interruptions prevent her from reading more. In particular, reading is contrasted with spending time with her boyfriend. While Ms. Webster attests to enjoying reading, she explains that her boyfriend discourages her reading because she is "supposed to spend time" with him and "not read books." Like Mr. Sherwood's description above, being a reader is juxtaposed with being social. Pursuing her desire to read requires Ms. Webster to isolate herself and risk annoying her boyfriend.

Despite Ms. Webster's statement that she will "go in the kitchen or in the bedroom and read" she still does not consider herself a bookworm.

> *Ms. Webster:* I mean cuz I love to read. And I never used to read when I was a kid. But you give me a book, a good book, and I'll sit there and read the book until it's done.
> *Ms. Lilly:* Do you consider yourself a bookworm or a . . .
> *Ms. Webster:* Bookish person? Mmm, no, no, not as much as a bookworm. But I like to read, I do. I mean I enjoy reading.

At the beginning of this chapter, Ms. Webster explained that real readers "don't have no fun." While Ms. Webster is willing to temporarily disrupt her social life to read, she does not view herself as a bookworm.

Four parents believe they definitely are not among those "certain people." Four others explain they like to read but qualified their response with a comment similar to Ms. Johnson's, "when I get a chance," or Ms. Mason's, "Well, sometimes when I have the time."

Ms. Rodriguez alone calls herself a reader, but she also qualifies her remarks by saying, "I have to be" based on her many years of continuing education. Yet in contrast to other participants who described reading as a solitary and isolating practice, Ms. Rodriguez re-creates the animated exchanges she has with her friends when they trade novels: "'Got a good novel?'" She laughs. "'Ahhh, did you read so and so? So and so?' 'No You got it?' 'Yeah. You should check it out.' 'Send it by so and so or I come and get it.'" Her comments are directed back to me again: "You know, stuff like that." Ms. Rodriguez believes that she is a real reader; she presents her experiences with reading very differently, emphasizing the social aspects of reading such as exchanging books and sharing opinions.

Despite their denials of being those certain people who are real readers, participants describe the important role reading has played in their lives. Participants show me novels they finished reading the night before and explain how reading has helped them in times of stress and challenge. Reading is something they can do and often enjoy, but it is not a central aspect of their identity. Those certain people who are real readers belong to another world, a professional world of loners who don't have any fun.

Ms. Green tells a particularly interesting story. While growing up she was part of a highly literate, White, middle-class, suburban family. Her mother was a teacher; her father had a master's degree. She describes her early years as a reader: "I liked the books. But the thing I found out, when you started reading um, you didn't have to be, here you are on your bed reading, you're off in India somewhere. That's what I liked." In terms of school, Ms. Green remarked, "That [school] was my thing. I liked going to school." However, as she explains in a halting and rather exasperated tone, "This is a long time ago. Ummm, I think, see, with me, I'm not sure, I mean it took, it took me so much just to keep um, I don't know. I can't spend my time reading, it, I can't even find anything, I don't know, man." Along with the social and economic changes that occurred in Ms. Green's life as a result of her mental illness came changes in her identity as a reader. As she stated, "In my past lives or whatever, I did a lot of reading"; and in a later interview, "But I don't know. I mean right now with me I just mostly watch TV."

Ms. Green acknowledges that she has plenty of time to read and cannot understand or explain why she does not read. Her identity as a reader was strong when she was surrounded by a middle-class literate environment but diminished greatly when her social and economic situation changed and her mental health declined. As a White woman living in a Black community Ms. Green remarks, "Of course half the time I think I'm Black anyhow"; this comment takes on a special significance when viewed in relation to the transition she has made from a suburban to an urban community. Not only has she physically moved into a new community, but she has also changed her identity around reading and around other fundamental aspects of her life. Ms. Green has also adopted behaviors and attitudes that reflect the cultural practices of the community in which she now resides.

In their study of literacy practices in Lancaster, England, Barton and Hamilton (1998) note that the people in their study did not equate reading the newspaper as real reading. This tendency was also noted in my research. Parents tended to view reading acts such as reading the newspaper, bingo books, magazines, and recipes as less authentic than reading books. When I asked Ms. Holt if she liked to read, she explained that she never liked to read and preferred sports. Knowing that she was an accomplished cook, I asked if she read recipes. "Yeah and I have to read those I guess. OK, OK, but reading was never something that I, you know, I don't know why. I'd rather, I didn't get the book I needed." Ms. Holt does not consider reading recipes as real reading. Reading and cooking are separate activities with real reading being associated with reading books, a school-like literacy activity, rather than with tasks she needs to accomplish in her daily life.

"The Worst Thing I Had in My Lifetime"

When parents discuss themselves as readers, they often tell stories about their school experiences. School and classroom practices affect people's attitudes about school, learning, and reading; the reading identities of the parents of my students are caught up in these school experiences. The words of parents recorded in this section suggest some of the ways in which parents have been taught that academic pursuits, including reading, are for people other than themselves.

As parents describe their experiences with school, several different themes arise that provide insight into possible reasons why parents do not view themselves as real readers. In the following section, I will present the words of parents who describe school as boring and reading as a solitary, sedentary activity. Parents talk extensively about teachers being unable to meet their needs. They describe being made to read particular books and teachers who are "stuck on the work" and uninterested in students as individuals.

Like Arlene Fingeret's (1982a, 1982b) adult students, many parents in this study describe school as "boring." As Kunjufu (1986) explains, the word *boring* is often used as a marker for other issues related to the inability of schools and teachers to challenge and engage youth. When schools fail to engage students and confirm their identities as learners, school learning, including reading, becomes defined as the property of "other" people. When school tasks, including reading, are experienced in this way, the identities of students are constructed in contrast to school rather than within the social expectations of the school.

Several parents comment on how schools, curricula, teachers and pedagogy fail to be interesting and relevant to students. Ms. Rodriguez suggests that teachers "find out what the kid is interested in." "Like he's [pointing to her high school–age son] more interested in music, in videos and stuff like that. I guess if it were something he was interested in, he wouldn't be so bored." Ms. Rodriguez advocates a child-centered pedagogy that takes into account students' interests. She recommends that teachers "find out" what children are interested in and use this information to guide instruction. Ms. Rodriguez then describes her own experiences in school. She explains, "Me personally, I liked novels and stuff like that, so if [you] want to make a child read just give them something that they like to read." She describes one of her sons who learned to read with comic books.

Ms. Webster suggests that teachers of younger children "make it [learning] like a game." Ms. Webster advocates a pedagogy that is engaging and entertaining. She recognizes that children love games and believes that schools can capitalize on this to prevent students from being bored.

Other parents describe reading itself as boring. Ms. Holt explains that to her reading is both sedentary and solitary. Ms. Holt contrasts herself and Bradford with her older children: "I'd never even think of reading a book that thick, with a thousand pages. I mean they'd [her older children would] just sit hours and hours and just read. Bradford sit that long? I guess he can't sit still that long. I guess." To Ms. Holt, reading a thousand pages means sitting still for a long time. The idea of sitting that long is not attractive to her. She expresses disbelief at her older children, who sit "hours and hours and just read." Her use of the phrase "just read" reveals her sense that rather than reading, they could be doing something else—perhaps something more productive, more interesting, or more fun.

Linda Brodkey describes a conflict that many non-middle-class children face, a conflict that "the middle-class practice of reading alone and in silence, only what is assigned, creates in a working-class child whose reading had until then [entering school], been part and parcel of the social fabric of the home" (Brodkey, 2000, p. 15). Such reading is a solitary and sedentary activity, in contrast to the purposeful and social reading that many children had the opportunity to encounter prior to entering school. As Ms. Holt described earlier, she does not consider reading recipes real reading and thus views these applied reading practices as less authentic than reading a book.

Similarly, Ms. Hudson recalls her frustration at having to sit in school; she describes how school was "more boring" in the summertime: "They be wanting to get out of there, play and do things." Being in school and school-related tasks are contrasted with other, more physically active things. As described in the previous section, parents often contrast the solitary and sedentary nature of reading with people's "real" lives and social relationships.

Parents also commented on the ways schools failed to meet their individual needs. Ms. Rodriguez found the regular work of the classroom to be too easy. Her teacher did not challenge her.

> *Ms. Rodriguez:* Them books was sooo easy and I used to breeze through them and then it's just like I said if she could be looking at me I'd be looking at her. And she's like, "So what are you up to?" "It's like you don't want to know. Can I get another book?"
>
> *Ms. Lilly:* So she let you go ahead at your own rate.
>
> *Ms. Rodriguez:* Yeah. Then she let me go at my own speed cuz she knew anything, I was bored and she was trying to keep my interest but it wasn't working.

The basal reading books were too easy; as she read through these books, her teacher simply brought her the next basal reader to complete. However, being allowed to read ahead was not enough to challenge Ms. Rodriguez; reading ahead did not keep her interest or engage her personally. While Ms. Rodriguez was successful with reading, she was not personally and purposefully engaged in school reading tasks. School reading was not connected to her life or her own purposes for reading. Because reading experiences at school demonstrated to her the separateness of school reading and her own life, Ms. Rodriguez's identity as a reader was not constructed around school reading tasks; rather, her identity as a reader was constructed in contrast to school reading tasks.

Ms. Rodriguez is the one parent who described herself as a real reader. While her school reading tasks are described as imposed and obligatory, Ms. Rodriguez enjoys a personal reading life that is grounded in social relationships and personally satisfying experiences with books.

Ms. Holt describes how she liked school but disliked the "reading part." "I didn't like it cuz it was hard, I guess it was the reading part that I didn't understand. You know so it made it difficult." At our first interview, Ms. Holt explained that she did not remember much about learning to read. Although she knew that she never enjoyed reading, she recalled very few details. Ms. Holt's involvement in these interviews inspired her to talk with her older sister about reading. Her sister reminded her that Ms. Holt had had difficulty learning to read. Ms. Holt explains that she had forgotten how difficult it had been.

> Yeah, yeah, I was asking [my sister] about how I was when I was young. She said, "Amanda, you know when you were coming up your reading never was that good, you know." I said, "Really?" She said, "Remember?" This was locked inside there [motions to her heart]. I say "OK, I remember those days." . . . Couldn't try to make me read and I just, you know. I guess they don't have the programs now as they had you know back, we're talking 30, 40 years ago.

Attesting to the trauma of her early reading experiences, Ms. Holt describes not remembering; it was "locked inside" her heart while the people around her were not able to "make" her read. Ms. Holt describes the frustration that arose from that experience.

For both Ms. Holt and Ms. Rodriguez, teachers and the curriculum were unable to meet their individual needs. However, participants also suggest that particular pedagogical approaches contributed to the development of negative reading identities. Just as Ms. Rodriguez was expected to read the basal textbook, Ms. Holt describes reading assigned books.

> I didn't like to read that much. That's what I'm saying it is nothing that I really enjoy doing and I don't, you know, I knew certain books when we were going to school that you had to read. Like *Shane* and *Old Yeller* and those you know back in my days were the books. [laughs] Well I'm just saying that I read them and had to write a book report on them and that was it.

When asked why she doesn't like to read, Ms. Holt spoke of being "made to read" these required books. To Ms. Holt, learning to read entailed people making her do things—making her learn and making her read "certain books." She wonders if perhaps she "didn't get the book" she needed; if Ms. Holt had been allowed to choose some of the books she read at school or if teachers had made connections between school texts and her life, perhaps Ms. Holt would have experienced reading as personally relevant. Instead, she was made to read particular books and respond to them in particular ways (for example, writing book reports).

Mr. Sherwood describes how school created reading difficulties for him that his mother, who is a teacher, has helped him overcome.

> The worst thing I had in my lifetime was when I used to be at the school. You know, they used to have the seats split up on this side, on this side people be studying [motions with his arm to one side] and the ones that couldn't read that good was on this side [motions to the other side] and they [those who could read] were on this side. So um, you know you had the, um the teacher, [we] used to get up and read it [the book] in front of all those people. You know you'd come out and say "Ahhh, man" [when you did not do well]. Especially when you get to the words that you don't even know, that was what hurts you know. And he'd [referring to himself] try to figure it out you know, that hurts real bad.

Mr. Sherwood refers to learning to read in school as the "worst thing I had in my lifetime." He was made to sit on the side of the room with other children who couldn't read. Like the other children, he was periodically asked to read in front of the class; this "hurting feeling" has never left Mr. Sherwood. Mr. Sherwood described this classroom in an earlier interview; he explained that the teachers "just put the book in front of me and they said go on read."

According to Mr. Sherwood, the teachers did not work with the children, instruct the children, or help the children; the children were just expected to read. When the other children could read and Mr. Sherwood could not, Mr. Sherwood explains, "That hurts real bad." The teacher and the classroom practices demonstrated to Mr. Sherwood that reading was not for him; he was seated among the nonreaders and little effort was made by the teacher to help him learn. Although Mr. Sherwood explains that thanks to his mother, he reads "pretty good now," the stories he tells about himself as a young reader continue to revolve around his initial school experiences with reading.

From the perspective of participants, it appears that schools have done things to demonstrate to parents that reading is not for them. Ms. Rodriguez was not challenged. Ms. Holt was forced to read books that were unrelated to her life or interests. Mr. Sherwood was physically placed with children who could not read and was just handed the book.

At other points in the interviews, Ms. Holt, Ms. Rodriguez, and Mr. Sherwood describe times when reading was enjoyable to them and they did learn to read. Ms. Holt describes choosing books from the bookmobile and reading them. Mr. Sherwood explains that despite his early experiences he did learn to read, "cuz you know I can pick it up now. After a while I picked it up . . . I think I'm pretty good now." Ms. Rodriguez enjoys sharing books with her friends. Reading itself was not always a negative experience, but reading in school was painful. When reading is presented this way in their classrooms, it is not surprising that parents do not identify themselves as real readers.

"She Was Stuck on Her Work"

Although Ms. Hudson describes her own experiences in school as boring, she attributes being bored to the students' attitude. "The kids' gonna be bored if they gonna be bored. You know it's not the teacher, it's the kid." Ms. Hudson adopts mainstream discourses about urban students that suggest that the difficulties they face are individual problems. If she was bored in school, it was not the fault of the teacher or the school; it was her own problem.

However, the majority of parents disagreed. They felt that teachers play a critical role in children's school experiences. Ms. Hernandez talks about what could have prevented her from dropping out of high school: "Maybe if the teachers like more get into it with the students or something. Maybe it would have been better. Cuz some of the classes were boring." Ms. Hernandez's words are couched in possibilities; "maybe" things would have been different. Like Ms. Rodriguez and Ms. Webster, she suggests that teachers get to know their students more, capitalize on students' interests, and make learning more enjoyable.

As described in Chapter Four, Ms. Webster explains that some teachers focus on the work rather than on the children. She describes these teachers as being "stuck on the work."

> Some teachers you know, they, they make it, some teachers can be like stuck on the work, you know. But the other teachers make it fun for the kids to learn. And when they feel it's fun to learn that's when you know they try to pick it up. . . . There's certain ways that teachers can really make a child, you know, want to learn.

Being stuck on the work is contrasted with making learning fun for children. When teachers are stuck on the work, there is a focus on content and completing instructional tasks rather than on children as individuals. Ms. Webster explains that teachers can "make a child . . . want to learn." When the work is fun and the child likes the teacher, they want to learn. For Ms. Webster, the teacher is the critical variable that will affect whether or not children enjoy school and learn.

As described in Chapter Three, many parents valued teachers who stay on the kids. Parents believe that this is the teachers' obligation. Ms. Johnson describes some of her older children's high school teachers:

> Well, I know at Washington [a local high school] a lot of the teachers just don't care. You know they're there to do a job and if the kids don't take advantage of what they are doing then that's not their problem. And I've actually had a couple of them say that.

Ms. Johnson notes that some teachers simply do their job and expect children to take advantage of what they offer. She describes these as teachers who do not care. Whether or not students' learn is not their problem; they have done their job.

CONCLUSION

This chapter began with Ms. Webster describing people who read all the time as being "bookworms" who "don't have no fun." She denies being a bookworm herself, although a later interview captures her sneaking into the kitchen to read at night and explaining that when she finds a good book she will "sit there and read the book until it's done." However, mainstream discourses as well as personal experiences with school reading may have contributed to Ms. Webster's reluctance to define herself a real reader.

Being a real reader entails more than enjoying reading or reading a lot. Within this particular discourse community, real reading involves particular ways of "using language, thinking, feeling, believing and acting" (Gee, 1990, p.143) and reading alone does not qualify someone as a member of this discourse community. This chapter revealed several mainstream discourses that relate to urban people's identities as readers.

"Real" readers are certain types of people. Being a "real" reader involves particular ways of thinking, acting, and interacting.

Urban parents generally distinguish themselves from this type of person.

Reading newspapers, bingo books, and magazines is not "real" reading. Real reading is generally defined as a solitary activity that involves reading books.

Learning to read is a liberating experience. The process of learning how to read provides people with new opportunities and possibilities. However, the data presented here reveals how the process of learning to read was often a discouraging and negative experience.

Covering curriculum is the goal of teaching. If a teacher instructs the children in all the required topics, he or she has done an adequate job. This discourse denies the importance of relationships as described in previous chapters.

Alan Block (2000) describes how the process of learning to read can make people feel inadequate. The prospect of having to read and say all the words correctly can be a frightening experience that can stay with people for many years. In addition, instructional activities that are not suited to the needs and interests of children demonstrate to the children that reading is not for them.

Learning to read and the formation of reading identities occur within social fields that are characterized by tensions created between mainstream and alternative discourses. Furthermore, in the process of learning to read most children will come into contact with people at both home and school who will be differentially positioned within social fields that incorporate both mainstream and alternative discourses about reading. While teachers and school personnel may not have experienced great degrees of disparity between mainstream discourses and their own lives, the lived experiences of urban families may often be at odds with mainstream interpretations of the world. For these families, alternative discourses may be more prevalent. Figure 6.1 presents a hypothetical social field in which the teacher and other school personnel appear on the right side of the figure based on their relatively strong investment in mainstream discourses; parents and some peers are positioned to the left because of their investment in alternative ways of viewing the world.

In the previous chapters, I explored the ways that parents and students understand the role of reading in their lives and the ways in which

Figure 6.1. A Positioning of Participants in Home and School Contexts

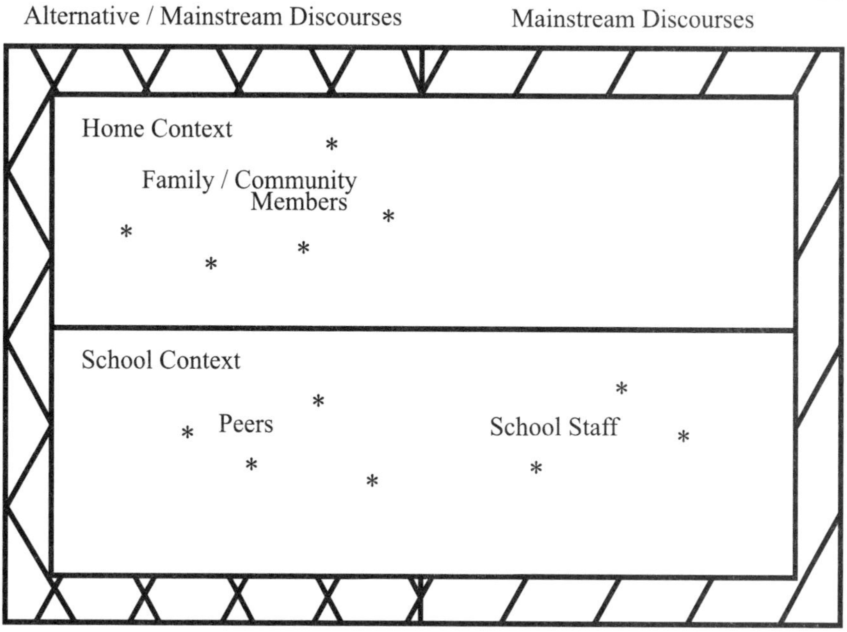

Alternative / Mainstream Discourses   Mainstream Discourses

Home Context   *

    Family / Community
        Members   *

  *   *   *

      *

School Context

          *   *

  * Peers   School Staff   *

    *   *   *

personal relationships can support or hinder the process of learning to read. In this chapter, we have heard the parents describe themselves as readers and contextualized these descriptions within their lives and experiences. In Chapter Seven, I will examine contradictions and complexities that are evident when the words of parents and children are voiced alongside mainstream discourses about urban families and reading.

7

Contradictions and Complexities

"[Young people who can't read] ain't trying to learn nothing."
"[Schools] just pass children along."
"She really packed it [reading] down on him."
"Their parents aren't helping them."
"Oh, I stay on them [my children]."
"They [the neighbor's children] take care of themselves all day."
"Get on him, get on him, he needs that." (Spoken to the teacher)
"They love her [the teacher] for it [being tough]."
"I've always been surrounded by books."
"Sound it out. You know your letters."
"If it wasn't for her [his mother] . . . "
"She [the teacher] goes to school and knows how to do it the right
    way."
"[Bookworms] don't have no fun."
"I love to read."
"I'd never even think of reading a book that thick."
"Got a good novel?"

The preceding chapters have presented a cacophony of voices—
different ideas, different understandings, different strategies, and different experiences all contributing to the rich variety of views and attitudes
on the part of parents and children in this study. However, it is essential not to reduce these differences to personal opinions, individual attitudes,
or personal choices. As Bakhtin explains, the word is not neutral; "it exists
in other people's mouths, in other people's contexts, serving other people's
intentions" (Bakhtin, in Morris, 1994, p. 78). All speech has a history of
being spoken in particular contexts by particular people with particular
purposes. We speak not with our own personal independent voices but
with the echoes of those whose words we have adopted and adapted and
whose ideological understandings continue to inhabit those words.

This is particularly true of mainstream discourses. In their natural-ized, taken-for-granted state, mainstream discourses obfuscate their ideo-logical meanings as well as their often clandestine connections to institu-tionalized power structures. While the parents in my study, and the teachers at my school (including myself), may not recognize the ideologi-cal assumptions implicit in our words nor the discourses connected to those words, these institutionally sanctioned ways of understanding the world are being supported and upheld through our unknowing subscrip-tion to mainstream discourses. As Bakhtin maintains, "We encounter it [the authoritative word] with its authority already fused to it" (Bakhtin, in Morris, 1994, p. 78).

A careful analysis of the comments that opened this chapter reveals a great degree of contradiction among the statements. While one voice reports that "[young people who can't read] ain't trying to learn nothing," another blames schools for "just pass[ing] children along." While parents believe that their neighbors "aren't helping" their children with learning to read, they report differently about themselves; "I stay on them." Throughout the interviews, contradictory voices would often be expressed by the same individual. The left column of Figure 7.1 lists several of the mainstream discourses about reading voiced by participants in this study;

Figure 7.1. A Sampling of Mainstream and Alternative Discourses

A Sampling of Mainstream Discourses About Reading	A Sampling of Alternative Discourses About Reading
Learning to read will significantly contribute to attaining a good job.	Getting a good job depends on who you know and circumstances in your life.
Unemployed people are unemployed because they do not apply themselves and have a poor attitude.	The system prevents many people from finding work that pays a living wage.
Reading is necessary for driving a car.	Some people drive cars without knowing how to read.
Poverty does not affect children as they learn to read.	Poverty affects everything.
Crime, violence, and dangerous communities do not affect children as they learn to read.	Crime, violence, and fear can affect children as they learn to read.
Reading for enjoyment is important.	Daily struggles for survival can prevent people from reading for enjoyment.

the right column lists alternative discourses raised by this same group of individuals. These alternative discourses reveal times when the lived experiences of participants fail to support mainstream discourses. Alternative discourses are then invoked. Fairclough (1989) refers to the construction of alternative discourses as "creative" processes (p. 165) that people use to make sense of their life experiences.

In this chapter, contradictions that arose during the research process will be presented and explored. First, I will present several mainstream discourses that parents challenge by putting forth alternative interpretations grounded in their own experiences. Next, I will examine the hesitancy with which parents raise and discuss explanations grounded in alternative discourses. Finally, I will investigate the potential of alternative discourses to effect and define social change.

CHALLENGING AND SUPPORTING MAINSTREAM DISCOURSES

In this section, I will present three mainstream discourses that parents voiced during the research project. First, I will introduce a discourse that promotes reading as critical for getting a good job and then describe challenges raised by parents. Second, I will present a discourse that emphasizes the importance of reading for driving, along with challenges to that discourse. Finally, I will complicate the argument by presenting a mainstream discourse that depicts urban parents as being uninterested in reading, challenge that discourse based on parents' sincere interest in reading, and then suggest an alternative explanation offered by parents for not reading regularly.

"That's a Tough One:" Reading and Getting a Good Job

Some parents challenge the direct relationship between learning to read and getting a good job by referring to other contingencies unrelated to education or reading ability. Marvin's grandfather, who explained that without learning to read, young people would only be able to get "garbage jobs," also talks about the limited effect that learning to read can have on one's gaining viable employment.

> I know a lot of people. They was um, that we have nothing but uh, and they love to read. Mmm-mm, they don't have no problem with that, but they have fun [reading]. The only problem with that is they read and they did their math and you know what upset them is that um, you get mad when they read and they figure that

all that they have, all the abilities and they can't get a job they get mad. They just get frustrated. 'Cause when I lost my job down there, I got frustrated . . . 'cause I was out there for 4 years. I said well I guess it ain't going to come, you know.

As Mr. Sherwood explains, reading is not a problem for him or many of his peers. The people he describes learned to read and did what was expected in school but when they are still unable to find work they become frustrated. The mainstream discourse that associates learning to read with employment has failed them.

Mr. Sherwood describes how he got his current job after 2 years of unemployment.

> Well, he [a friend] just knew this person and I know [him], you know. I don't know how I got in. Someone liked me and hired me. You see a lot of kids come out of school that way [with the necessary skills but no job]. See you know they are very, very smart kids. You know they get frustrated when they can't [get a job], you know. And I, I don't blame them.

Despite his insistence that reading is essential, reading only played a minor role in his own success with getting a job. As he explained, "Someone liked me and hired me."

Ms. Rodriguez agrees with Mr. Sherwood. She spoke with certainty, "Uh, it's like *who you know*." Ms. Rodriguez explained how her husband "got in somewhere good" (a job entering data into computers) when her husband's best friend got him an application and "moved it [the application] up."

Christy's mother laughed aloud when I suggested that reading might guarantee a good job. Her personal struggle with bipolar disorder has left her poignantly aware of the variables that can complicate securing a good job:

> [Laughing] The things that guarantee a good job are a whole lot of circumstances in your life. You could have the best, the best um education. You could have a master's or whatever, higher than that and if you have certain things in your life that will fuck you up like alcoholism, anything you know the routine there.

Ms. Green was a gifted student from a small, middle-class community who graduated from high school at age 16 and continued on to college until she became mentally ill. Ms. Green's case may be unique, but as she describes, there are many reasons besides literacy that prevent people from securing a good job.

All the parents I interviewed expressed confidence in their ability to read; however, three participants were unemployed and most others were working at minimum-wage jobs. It is these lived experiences that disrupt the mainstream discourses that associate being able to read with viable employment, and lead to the creation of alternative discourses to explain the limited role that reading actually plays in attaining employment.

"It's Strange. He Couldn't Read:" Reading and Driving a Car

Contradictions are also evident in the ways parents describe reading as essential for driving a car. Parents emphasize the importance of reading for driving and at the same time contradict themselves by telling remarkable stories about people who drive professionally without knowing how to read. Ms. Allan, Ariana's foster grandmother, describes how she drove a school bus for many years despite her "problem with reading" and never having finished elementary school. Ms. Holt explains how her stepfather drove a truck for years without knowing how to read:

> It's strange. He couldn't read but he was a truck driver. Anywhere in the city that he had to go he knew. But he used to, my mother would map it out. They'd both be sitting down. She'd map out where he had to go 'cause he, he would know the day before where he was going to go the next day. He'd come home and he'd hurry to get on that table and they'd map out his route and tell him where to go and show him the letters. 'Cause she taught, she taught him the different letters and little [things like] how to sign his name.

Ms. Holt's words reflect a mainstream discourse about needing to read in order to drive that is powerful enough for her to find it strange that her stepfather could drive a truck without knowing how to read. However, these compelling and intriguing examples of individuals who have defied this mainstream discourse point not only to the resilience of these individuals but also to the fact that driving may not require the amount of reading that people assume it does. Most signs are comprehensible on the basis of shape and color, alleviating the need to read the words. One can generally discern street signs, as Ms. Holt's stepfather does, through attention to letters and salient features.

The importance of these allusions to the relationship between reading and driving lies not in its accuracy; of importance is the ways parents reference driving as evidence for the importance of learning to read. As the examples described here reveal, people can drive and get around with limited reading skills.

"I Used to Like to Read Books:" Reading and Not Reading

While mainstream discourses characterize urban parents as illiterate or aliterate, parents' stories presented in Chapter Three attest to the interest and enjoyment many parents in this study associate with reading. However, several parents lament that they no longer read regularly because of the stresses and strains of their daily lives. Ms. Horner explains that the demands of parenthood have made it difficult for her as a single mother to find time to read: "I feel guilty because, um, to be perfectly honest since I've had my children I have not read a book, since I had my kids. I used to like to read books all the time. I had so many books."

Ms. Green explains that because of taking care of a critically ill boyfriend for the past year and dealing with her ongoing mental health problems, she rarely reads. Her present emphasis is on survival.

> I don't know what it is. Um, I, I, in a way it's like I think I got to survive, just basically survive. And the only ways to do it right now is just to basically feed my basic needs and stuff. And maybe it is just one thing too much to read, to try to like [read] to Christy or anybody else . . . cause the psyche is too weak.

While parents describe the importance of personal reading in their lives, some parents find that the pressures of daily life prevent them from reading as much as they would like. Thus, there is a tension between the value they place on reading and the demands and pressures of their lives. They regret not being able to read more often. Some of the parents of my students do not read regularly, but it is not because they do not enjoy and value reading; rather the stresses and pressures of their lives make finding time to read difficult.

"I DON'T KNOW:" THE LIMITS OF ALTERNATIVE DISCOURSES

In this section, I will present four occasions in which parents offer explanations grounded in alternative discourses to explain situations in their lives. Each time these alternative discourses are invoked, parents hesitate and express a lack of confidence in their words. This hesitancy is not unique to the four stories presented in this section. Throughout this book, hesitancy and a lack of confidence is evident in the words of parents as they put forth explanations that challenge mainstream interpretations of the world. First, I will explore the way one parent describes factors that affect employment opportunities. Then, I will present three aspects of parenting in an urban community and examine the ways parents talk about the effect these situations might have on children learning to read.

It's the System

Mr. Sherwood highlights the contradictory relationship between education and employment. He explains how people in his community view "the system" and the role it plays in securing employment:

> Sometimes they [his peers] figure that 12th grade, they figure that [they have] a high school diploma, I'm gonna go get a good job. And it don't, and it don't happen. That didn't come, so they, they figure the, it, they figure that the system, the system messed me around. That's their figuring right here. But it's not the system. . . . You know I've had an attitude problem myself, but you know and it's, it's no good at all. Cause I figure I'm getting all this and I went to trade school. I did this you know and all of a sudden I ain't gonna have nothing, and I said naw this ain't going to happen like this so I took another route. I didn't go that pathway, you know.

Mr. Sherwood explains that he completed trade school but suddenly found himself with "nothing" when the company he worked for shut down. However, like the African American men interviewed by Fine and Weis (1998), instead of centering his critique on the job market or the lack of viable opportunities for urban, non-White, residents, Mr. Sherwood challenges those who blame the system, citing the importance of personal accountability: he explains, "I've had an attitude problem myself." By emphasizing personal accountability, Mr. Sherwood supports mainstream discourses that blame the poor for their own problems. Mr. Sherwood clearly explains that the problem is more related to attitude than to the system; he describes the attitude of people around him and the need to "deal with it yourself":

> They get discouraged then they say the system owes them something and all, they want to take off, take on the system and all that um, and "if I had a chance, I could do that." I hear this stuff all the time. You know, no, ain't nobody owe you nothing. You do,

I'll tell you, do it yourself. You got to deal with it yourself. You know, you got all the opportunities.

However, when asked why the people in this community have difficulties finding good jobs, Mr. Sherwood paused. "That's a tough one. That's a tough one right there. Cause um, I've been sitting trying to figure that one out." Then, contradicting what he said about the importance of personal attitude and having to "do it yourself" he concedes, "See, the system's not working for them."

This brief exchange provides an example of an alternative discourse that cites the system as an alternative reason for unemployment rather than poor job skills, limited reading abilities, or poor attitudes. However, Mr. Sherwood dismisses that alternative discourse, adopting a mainstream discourse based on appropriate attitude, while still acknowledging that the mainstream discourse fails to account for the employment difficulties of the people he knows.

Mainstream discourses fail to account for the difficulties of people in this community; however, alternative discourses locate blame within the larger system but do not have access to a means of addressing the larger system or even to discourses of critique that are recognized within the larger society. Throughout this conversation and in subsequent interviews, Mr. Sherwood never defines *the system*; even when asked directly, he simply confirms its existence.

Mr. Sherwood's words express a contextualized negotiation that is spoken through a combination of mainstream and alternative discourses. There is a lack of viable opportunities for voices of poor, underemployed city residents, like Mr. Sherwood's, to be heard against the deafening din of mainstream discourses. Without the ability to voice alternative discourses effectively, Mr. Sherwood advocates clinging to the mainstream discourse, with faith that jobs are out there and confidence that his peers can manage those positions. However, as his words suggest, "that's a tough one." Mr. Sherwood clearly recognizes the limits of the mainstream discourse to effectively explain and address his difficulties and the difficulties of his peers.

Ms. Webster, who earlier supported the mainstream discourse when she explained that it was important for her daughter Tiffany to learn to read, in order to be able to fill "out an [job] application," tries to explain the inability of her European American peers to get decent jobs. Ms. Webster grew in a rural upstate area. When asked why young people who did well in high school had trouble after graduation, she replied, "I don't know. It's like after high school, it's just, I don't know. They, they get all their [unclear word] and they change up. It's just like they give up, don't care." Like Mr. Sherwood, Ms. Webster describes how success in school fails to translate into success in the outside world. Although Ms. Webster explains that she doesn't know what contributes to these difficulties, she adopts a mainstream discourse that identifies an attitude problem; people "just don't care." Ms. Webster clearly struggles to make sense of this situation; she seems to be attempting to identify other factors that affect her peers' difficulty in getting jobs, but is left with only "attitude." Ms. Webster uses the phrase *I don't know* twice.

The phrase *I don't know* is particularly revealing. Throughout the research project this phrase signaled times when parents were unable to reconcile their own experiences and the alternative discourses grounded in those experiences with mainstream discourses about reading and education.

It's Not Poverty

While mainstream discourses suggest that being poor affects children's ability to learn to read, several parents I interviewed report that being poor has nothing to do with learning to read; however, as parents challenged these mainstream discourses, they also expressed uncertainty. When asked if poverty affected children learning to read, Ms. Hudson responded, "No, I don't think so." When asked why she felt it did not, she responded, "I just, I don't know, I just figure it doesn't." Ms. Horner reports that being on welfare "should have no effect at all" on children's ability to learn to read. Ms. Holt agrees:

> 'Cause, you know why? Because the kids that have nothing, they have time to do anything but [what they have] time [to] do is read. The [rich] kids have these Nintendo games; these kids have the best of everything. They don't have time to do nothing but play. But a child that has nothing will pick up a book just as entertainment, see? That's my personal opinion.

These alternative discourses are couched in words that convey the speakers' uncertainty ("I don't know," "I just figure," "personal opinion").

It's Not Poor Parenting

Parents also challenge mainstream discourses positing poor parenting as the cause of children's difficulties with reading. Many parents describe how friends and neighbors work with their own children and support their children as they learn to read. Ms. Holt reports that even parents who use drugs are not necessarily detrimental to their children's ability to read.

> I don't know, you know. It is very hard to say that, I know, I know people that you know, that I know that do it [do drugs], but they sit down with their kids and make them do their homework with them so, I just can't really say that that causes it either because one of my, my best friend she's one of them [unclear] but when it's time for her daughter to do her homework she's right there on her, makes her do that homework, and she do the best she can with her, you know—so, I can't really say.

As Ms. Holt reports, even under the most negative circumstances, parents can and often do manage to do the "best they can" for their children. Again, however, Ms. Holt does not know this for certain, explaining, "It is very hard to say."

It's Not Feeling Safe

Factors other than parental neglect were often cited as being related to children's difficulties with reading. While the mainstream discourses blame parents for the reading difficulties of children, Ms. Holt points to another possible cause but again situates her words within a discourse of not knowing.

> Like when I was coming up we could go outside this time of the day and just play and you know not worry about someone coming by in a drive-by, didn't have to worry about gang fare. All these different things. You know, it was kinda, I felt secure. I don't know, I don't know if he [Bradford] feels safe when he's out there or not. You know what I'm saying. I don't let him go too far but I'm just saying when he's away, I don't know how, how does he feel? Safe? Home or not, I don't know if that has an effect on him, some learning abilities or not so, you know, so . . .

Ms. Holt uses the phrase *I don't know* four times. It is this unknown, the suspected but unconfirmed, alternative discourse that challenges the mainstream discourse.

Similarly, I asked Ms. Mason if gangs affect children's ability to learn to read. She replied, "I'm not sure. That question, I leave it blank." She then commenced to tell a story about a little boy in her neighborhood who was pursued by a gang of boys. As her initial comments imply,

Ms. Mason suspects that there may be a relationship between children treating each other poorly and children having trouble learning to read. However, the specific nature of this relationship remains unspoken; as Fine and Weis explain, it is difficult "for those inside the group to have confidence in their judgments over time, to have those judgments be anything more than angry stabs at American society" (1998, p. 65).

ALTERNATIVE DISCOURSES AND SOCIAL CHANGE

I also experience uncertainty when I challenge mainstream discourses at my school. When I describe the parents in my study, my colleagues dismiss me, insisting that most of the parents at our school are not like the ones I interviewed. When I explain that the families in my study were randomly selected, they respond, "Well, most of the parents of my students . . . " and the rest of the sentence is completed with "don't care," "can't read," "don't read," or some other judgment based on the parents' perceived incompetence. At this point in the conversation my own words and my data fail me. The number of people I interviewed is too small to confront the unshakable opinions of my peers. As my colleagues deny the possibility of other ways of viewing the families in our school community, they maintain the dominance of mainstream discourses. Just as the parents of my students experience a point at which they lose confidence in what they know and have experienced, teachers and researchers are subject to a lack of words to convey alternative discourses that effectively challenge the dominance of mainstream ways of viewing urban students and their families.

What does this tendency of people, including myself, to lose confidence in alternative discourse when challenged by dominant ways of thinking mean for teachers, parents, and students in urban schools? Is a discourse of possibilities possible within a society in which naturalized and entrenched mainstream discourses support existing power structures and deny the existence of alternative ways of viewing the world? Is there hope for addressing the dominance of mainstream discourses in schools and society? Despite my personal frustrations and the apparent hesitancy of my students' parents, the very existence of alternative discourses presents the possibility of change.

Educators must understand that discourses that support established, formal institutions are valued above narratives grounded in the experiences of people. As Fairclough (1995) explains,

> There are structures and mechanisms for privileging the judgments
> of particular social groups and the particular discourses they deploy,

> including intellectuals. An important emancipatory political objective is to minimize such effects and maximize the conditions for judgments of truth to be compared and evaluated on their own merits. (1995, p. 19)

Dell Hymes suggests that the existence of contradictory voices presents the possibility of change and that positive change could result from listening to others outside the mainstream: "It would be fitting if recognition of the interest and richness of narratives from the margins should come to transform the whole" (1996, p. xii).

However, the ways in which mainstream discourses and alternative discourses based on narratives from the margins portray the world often emerge as contradictory, with alternative discourses being flagged by statements of uncertainty and questioning. As Bakhtin recognizes and the voices of the parents of my students demonstrate, alternative discourses are difficult to formulate and express.

> Unofficial aspects of consciousness are also historically and socially determined by what any particular society sanctions or censors. However, what is unofficial cannot be so fully formulated and expressed even in inner speech. (Bakhtin, in Morris, 1994, p. 9)

Thus, while alternative discourses challenge mainstream discourses, they also defy clear articulation. Nevertheless, challenges to mainstream discourses result in the surfacing of "lines of tension" (Fairclough, 1993, p. 68) between the dominant mainstream discourses and alternative discourses. In my research, lines of tension evolved constantly as parents both cited and challenged mainstream discourses.

It must be remembered that discourses, including mainstream discourses, are not static and unchanging. "The ideological environment is constantly in the active dialogical process of generation. Contradictions are always present, consistently being overcome and reborn" (Bakhtin, in Morris, 1994, p. 127). This eternal state of discoursal struggle ensures the eternal possibility of change. Fairclough (1995) explains that when "contradictory positions overlap they provide a basis for awareness and reflexivity, just as they lead to problemization and change" (p. 82). He explains that "change leaves traces in texts in the form of co-occurrence of contradictory or inconsistent elements" (p. 79), evident in the contradictory words of the parents of my students. Thus, the contradictions revealed in my research suggest that a change process has been initiated; yet the hesitancy and lack of confidence expressed by parents indicate that substantial change is not imminent.

A critical element remains to be clearly established within this community: "The effectiveness of resistance and realization of change depend on people developing a critical consciousness of domination and its modalities rather than just experiencing them" (Fairclough, 1989, p. 4). For example, Mr. Sherwood identifies "the system" as a factor in the difficulties his peers face in getting jobs. Ms. Holt wonders if her children's concerns about safety affect them as they learn to read. Yet Mr. Sherwood did not define *the system* and Ms. Holt did not explain how fears related to safety are related to reading. Thus a critical consciousness that enables my students, their parents, and others in their communities to recognize, name, and challenge domination is not yet fully articulated (Freire, 1986).

Despite their silences, Bakhtin provides words of hope: "One's own discourse and one's own voice, although born of another or dynamically stimulated by another, will sooner or later begin to liberate themselves from the authority of the other's discourse" (Bakhtin, in Morris, 1994, p. 79). Perhaps our best hope as teachers is to seek ways to accelerate the process. One way to do this is by working with families to create what Gee (1992) refers to as "borderlands" that are situated between home and school and feature a hybrid discourse that merges home and school discourses.

Kris Gutierrez and colleagues refer to this hybrid context as a "third space" in which "alternative and competing discourses and positionings transform conflict and difference into rich zones of collaboration and learning" (Gutierrez, Baquedano-Lopez, & Tejeda, 1999, p. 287). While Gutierrez and her colleagues explore instances of "third space" construction within classrooms, my research suggests that teachers, students, and parents would benefit from participating in third spaces that merge home and school literacy and learning practices and perspectives. Teacher research that extends beyond the classroom door, involves parents, and entails understandings of the lived experiences of students and their families has the potential to lead to the creation of spaces in which teachers can learn about their students, challenge their own assumptions, and ultimately construct learning experiences that value, reflect, and build upon the rich literate heritages of urban students.

CONCLUSION

As mainstream discourses collide and conflict with the experiences of my students and their families, the parents of my students have constructed alternative discourses that present alternative interpretations of their worlds. While mainstream discourses locate the reading difficulties of poor urban children in their families' attitudes and lack of interest in their children as readers, my research demonstrates the importance that parents place on reading as a discourse of possibility and particularly as a means of "getting somewhere" in terms of employment, physical mobility, and escape from the demands of daily life. However, while voicing mainstream discourses, parents also invoke alternative discourses that challenge the direct relationship between reading and getting somewhere. These discourses cite complexities such as dealing with the system, "who you know," and children feeling safe in their own communities.

Perhaps most significant is the uncertainty that is expressed as parents invoke alternative discourses. Because alternative discourses challenge the naturalization of particular ideologies, they threaten well-entrenched, mainstream ways of viewing society and the people in it. Thus, the uncertainty of the parents of my students is understandable. Although parents often construct alternative discourses based on their own lived experiences, these discourses are subject to the ideological dominance of mainstream discourses and parents tend to display a lack of confidence in their own voices.

In the final chapter a case study of one family will be presented to explore both the contextualized model of reading that has been presented in this book and the ways a lack of various forms of capital can limit participants' access to resources and opportunities. Finally, recommendations for educators based on this research will be offered.

8

A Concluding Case Study

I'm so disgusted now with [what happened to] my son I could, I could just, when something like that happen, I could tell them [my younger children], oh, you don't have to go to school cuz this gonna happen to you when you get to 12th and you never knew a thing [you never saw it coming]. I could just make them be discouraged instead of [telling them] no, you're going to work through it.

Despite Ms. Holt's son having been on the honor role for his most recent report card, he was "pushed out" of school (Fine, 1991) in May of his senior year of high school and not allowed to graduate, without any explanation offered. Ms. Holt is clearly frustrated by the manner in which her older son's high school career has ended. She contemplates allowing her frustration to affect the ways she deals with her younger children but rejects this, although Ms. Holt's belief that doing well in high school will lead to a diploma has been shattered.

Despite this devastating experience, Ms. Holt refuses to allow her younger children to lose faith. She insists that they "work through it" without becoming discouraged in much the same way Mr. Sherwood insists that "you got to deal with it yourself" when his peers blame the system for their lack of employment opportunities. Ms. Holt and Mr. Sherwood are displaying remarkable degrees of resilience and modeling this resilience for their children. In these cases, resilience involves maintaining faith in mainstream explanations and practices despite life experiences that suggest such faith may be unwarranted. With a lack of other viable options, however, continued faith in mainstream discourses is a rational response.

In this chapter, I will share Ms. Holt's story in order to explore the ways Bradford's reading experiences are conceptualized within discourse communities that operate in his home, at school, and within the larger community. The experiences of Bradford, his mother, and his siblings demonstrate how concepts about reading are intertwined with lived experiences as well as the economic, social, and political contexts in which people live. The contextualized model of reading presented throughout this book will frame Ms. Holt's story.

BRADFORD'S FAMILY AND READING: APPLICATION OF A CONTEXTUALIZED MODEL

Bradford's mother, Ms. Holt, was particularly forthcoming in describing her life and the complexities that have defined her role as a mother. As a single parent of five children in high school and beyond as well as of Bradford and his brother, who both attend Rosa Parks Elementary School, Ms. Holt has watched her older children grow up and progress through school. Her experiences with the school district have ranged from supporting teachers in their discipline decisions to having a child placed in special education and later attempting to prevent the same son from being pushed out of school during his senior year.

Mainstream Discourses About Reading

Like other parents in this study, Ms. Holt voices several mainstream discourses about the importance of learning to read. She speaks adamantly and with passion about the need for Bradford to learn to read: "If he can't read he's not going to go anyplace in this world." She describes the role her mother played in making sure that Ms. Holt and her siblings finished high school: "She [her mother] wanted us to be something so I can understand that. We ain't nothing great but we got . . . school. And that was very important to her. That was." Ms. Holt also describes her teachers as keeping her on track: "I don't believe the word *can't* was in her [the teacher's] vocabulary."

However, when asked about her children and their experiences as readers, Ms. Holt recognizes a contradiction and struggles to make sense of it. Throughout the interviews she speaks with pride about her children's proclivity toward reading: "Like one of my twins, Jerry: he was reading since he was 4 years old. He just got the newspaper and just started reading it." She explains that her older children would "just sit hours and hours and just read." However, their educational and life trajectories deny their accomplishments as readers. As described in Chapter One, Ms. Bradford believes that something happened to her children in middle and high school that caused them to lose interest in reading and school. Ms. Holt's frustration is evident in her voice as she tries to explain the contradiction between their earlier interest in reading and the difficulties they face in middle and high school. She wonders if children lose interest or succumb to peer pressure; she punctuates her words with the phrases *I don't know* and *I have no idea,* revealing her struggle to make sense of the experiences of her children. For Ms. Holt, the mainstream discourse that associates learning to read with school success and eventually getting a good job have failed. Her older children are exceptional readers, yet this accomplishment has not led to its promised end. For this family, reading was not the economic salve it was promised to be. Her eldest son graduated from high school and was killed in a tragic DWI accident, her daughter dropped out of school, and her next eldest son, a special education student on the honor role, was in the process of being pushed out of school close to the end of his senior year.

Other contradictions punctuate the interviews. Ms. Holt insists that reading is essential for driving a car—"you can't go no places"—yet it is her father who drove a truck for years but never learned to read. Ms. Holt also emphasizes the need for parents to monitor their children but worries that she "hibernated" her older children too much. These contradictions are consistently accompanied by hesitancy and uncertainty: "I don't know" and "I have no idea."

Alternative discourses voiced by Ms. Holt attribute the difficulties of children to neglect by teachers who don't care, the urban environment, and children just losing interest in school as they move from elementary school through middle school and into high school. However, these discourses remain at the level of local critique and are not generally recognized by the larger society. Alternative discourses that associate getting a job with who you know or beating the system provide little support for struggling families. Both the mainstream discourses and alternative discourses have failed to provide Ms. Holt with possibilities for her children. Disjunctures that associate reading with success and not learning to read with not feeling safe in one's community, or that juxtapose the ability to drive a truck with illiteracy, challenge mainstream interpretations of the world. Ms. Holt is left frustrated and without access to a discourse that both is recognized within the mainstream community and reflects her lived experiences.

Figure 3.2, presented in Chapter Three, demonstrates how mainstream discourses voiced by Ms. Holt collide with the alternative explanations that she offers to make sense of her world. While the right side of the diagram reflects mainstream discourses minus alternative interpretations of reality, the left side of the diagram reflects the lived tensions that Ms. Holt and many urban parents confront on a daily basis as they attempt to reconcile their lived experiences with mainstream discourses. The contradictions and tensions that Ms. Holt experiences position her to the left side of Figure 3.2.

The Home Context

In Figure 4.1, the home experiences of students are superimposed on Figure 3.2. Some children's home experiences will align with mainstream discourses about what families do and how they function; these children and families will be positioned on the right side of the diagram. Other families and children will find truth and meaning in alternative discourses. In what follows, I will explore comments related to reading and Bradford's home experiences.

Ms. Holt grew up in a suburban area on the west side of our city. As she explains, "See back when I was raised up I wasn't raised up around no Blacks. My mother she kept us you know kind of distant . . . you know, she just didn't want us to get into gangs and get in all that trouble." She describes her mother as tough on her children and as not "going [for] that dropout stuff." Her mother was successful; Ms. Holt and all four of her siblings graduated from high school. Ms. Holt values this toughness and describes how she has monitored her own children. She describes the role her mother played in making certain that she learned to read: "[Being] poor has nothing to do with learning how to read or whatever. I'm poor, I'm just trying to make him [Bradford] to read. My mother always said she was poor; she used to be on us for us to read."

While Ms. Holt has stressed the importance of learning to read to her children, she describes herself as not being a reader: "I'm not a reader. Like some people say they're readers. I'm not one of them." However, she does report that she enjoys reading the newspaper as well as recipes when she cooks. She explains that Bradford, unlike his siblings, is a reluctant reader: "Bradford is kinda like me he doesn't really like to read." Although she reports that she often helps Bradford with his reading, as do his older brother and sister, she laments that she should help Bradford more:

> We sit and read whatever papers he bring home from school. We read them together. You know, I should make him read them over and over, but we read them once, or maybe twice and that's OK. Bradford go ahead [unclear] . . . go ahead, put it away . . . I should insist that he read more though.

Ms. Holt talks about "making" Bradford read more; when talking about her own school experiences, she was frustrated by teachers who "made" her read particular books. Later in the interviews, after speaking with her sister about learning to read and how difficult that was for Ms. Holt, Ms. Holt explains that "[teachers] couldn't try to make me read." This recurrence of the word *make* in relation to reading across interviews reveals Ms. Holt's idea that reading is something that students are made to do and in general not an enjoyable activity.

Despite her own reluctance toward reading, Ms. Holt struggles to explain Bradford's difficulties with reading. She considers that possibility that her own reluctance to read may be affecting Bradford but rejects that explanation:

> I can't say I blame it on myself but, you know, but he's good enough because his brother reads and his sister she used to read all the time. I mean even his other brother, the one who passed away, he read constantly. They'd get in their rooms for hours and hours and hours [with] those thick old, big old, big old books. [That's] something I never did.

Ms. Holt remains perplexed about Bradford's difficulties and offers other possibilities. She reports that they did visit a pediatrician to determine whether Bradford was dyslexic, "but we found out he wasn't that, thank God." She even wonders if a bad fall as a child might have affected Bradford's reading, but the doctors she consulted refuted that possibility also.

Finally, we must remember that the Holt family is situated within a poor community that suffers from a lack of resources. When I asked Ms. Holt if there are obstacles to learning to read in this community she expressed concern that the city was closing several libraries in the metropolitan area: "I think it's disgusting when I see them close up a library. And they talk about they want the kids to read and this and that." She talks about the need for bookmobiles or community houses where kids could get access to books. Ms. Holt criticizes the building of an additional police station rather than providing resources that will help children in school: "We don't need that many police. Listen the neighborhood is not that bad. It's kinda rough but come on now. Three police stations in two blocks. [Does] that make me think [that] I should be living over here? Is this that bad?" She explains, "They wonder why our kids [are] like they are. They need a little helping hand. They say it takes a community to raise a child. There's a community that needs help."

While people voice the importance of communities working together to support children, Ms. Holt does not believe that this is happening in her community. The local government is closing libraries and opening police stations. The decisions being made in her community focus on controlling people and consolidating expenses; Ms. Holt wants resources and opportunities for her children. While mainstream discourses blame Ms. Holt for the perceived deficiencies in her children, she suggests that the problems with reading in this community are more than personal problems.

The School Context

In Figure 5.3, the school experiences of students are superimposed on Figure 3.2 beneath the box depicting children's home experiences. As with their home experiences, some children's school experiences will align with mainstream discourses about reading and the role of families; these children and families will be positioned on the right side of the diagram. Other children and members of their families will challenge mainstream discourses about the role and value of reading. In this section, I will explore Bradford's school experiences.

Bradford entered my classroom in September with a student record that indicated that he had attended prefirst the year before in a nearby school. The prefirst program is designed for children who have been identified by their kindergarten teachers as potentially benefiting from an additional year of schooling prior to attending first grade. In prefirst, Bradford's reading program focused on decoding words. His mother explains,

> The "bib" [a strategy for sounding-out words] is the way they taught him to read last year and the teachers that taught him kinda taught me how [to do] it too. And we just "bib it." Like "walk"—you say "www . . . " and "luh-kuh" (Ms. Holt sounds out the word for me).

Despite Bradford's continuing difficulties with reading, Ms. Holt reports that this program works. She also describes with pleasure a pizza incentive program, although she reports that "it's a shame that you have to bribe kids to read." Unfortunately, curriculum that focuses on decontextualized skills and a reliance on extrinsic motivators are very common in urban schools where students are assumed to be deficit in both ability and motivation.

When Bradford entered my classroom in September, his reading ability was ahead of that of most of the other children in the classroom; however, as the year went on he fell behind, and by midspring he appeared frustrated and uninterested in reading. Because Bradford was a year older than the other children, he did not qualify for Reading Recovery services, which are targeted at 6-year-old children. The only services that were potentially available to Bradford were special education services, which required a formal referral. A referral was made that spring.

Although Bradford was not the only child in this study who struggled to learn to read, he appeared more frustrated than the other struggling students, perhaps because of his difficulties in the past and being a year older than the other children. He consistently referred to reading as "knowing words" and "sounding out words," explaining that learning to read "makes you smart." Bradford was the only child I interviewed who obviously did not enjoy the interview process; in the classroom, he tended to avoid any activity that involved reading unless he was enticed by his peers. At the final interview Bradford was particularly vexed that his mother made him stay home for the interview rather than letting him walk up to the corner store with his brother. He participated but gave short answers and physically moved away from me during the interview. He was anxious for the interview to end. Bradford's frustrations with learning to read made talking about reading a struggle.

Bradford's mother reports that despite his frustration, "he enjoys going to school. Yeah, believe it or not!" She describes him bringing happy faces and sad faces home from his math teacher.

> Some days he'll come in my room, sit on the bed, "What's wrong Bradford? . . . I said what's the matter?" Then he start explaining why he got that bad face cause he know I'm not having it. And me and him discuss when he had it and what we're not . . . going to do so we don't have one tomorrow. And we go on from there but he doesn't like those sad faces . . . 'cause he started getting them like every day.

When I asked about Bradford's older siblings and school, Ms. Holt didn't indicate any difficulties with reading but did report frustration: "Ohhh, Jesus Christ [with exasperation in her voice], those schools. I don't know. School was ho—, I don't know. They, they're disgusted with school."

Ms. Holt shares some of her children's frustrations. She relates a story about one of her older children. Apparently she had come in for a conference to discuss a problem her son was having at school and the school principal suggested that her son would be better off living with his father.

> He said, "When your, when your son was staying with his dad he was doing so much better. As a matter of fact how long has he

been back home?" I said, "What are you trying to insinuate? That I'm a bad mother?" I mean I got, I mean I got offensive [offended] right quick because he was only at his father's house maybe 6 weeks. And you try to tell me that since he's come back with me he's got that much of a change. I said no, that's not why. Then I went into detail why he changed and then he [the principal] made a total about-face but he had just made an assumption.

As Ms. Holt explains, the principal was quick to assume that the problem was her parenting. Ms. Holt challenges this and appears to have been successful in helping the principal to rethink his assumption. However, Ms. Holt was deeply offended by the assumptions that had been made and suggests that situations such as this one contribute to parents not feeling welcome in their children's schools.

In an earlier interview, Ms. Holt describes another meeting with a different principal concerning another child. Apparently a teacher had failed to follow through on an agreed-upon action,

I said remember when we [were] on the phone and you told me [you were going to do something]. And she just sat there and looked at me like this [demonstrates a blank stare]. But she never did say she was wrong. But the principal looked at her and he said, "Mmm-hmm. You said it and you didn't go along with it. I see why she's upset." But that was one of the better teachers [according to the principal].

Communication with the school has obviously been difficult at times for Ms. Holt. Assumptions precede her and agreements are not honored.

While mainstream discourses present schools as sanctuaries of hope, the experiences of Ms. Holt and her children reveal that they are instead often sites of conflict and tension. Reading is often presented as an activity of practicing decontextualized skills and something that requires a bribe to complete.

Bradford's Position

Although Bradford's mother ascribes to many mainstream discourses about the importance of reading and doing well in school, these discourses are challenged by the family's life experiences. In particular, knowing how to read has not proved to be the promised economic salve for Bradford's mother or his older siblings. While Ms. Holt continues to encourage Bradford to practice his reading and to work hard in school, Bradford is aware of the experiences of others in his family. Furthermore, Bradford's family lives in a community in which, despite official claims about the importance of learning to read, libraries are being closed and resources are scarce.

Bradford's brief school history included early reading experiences that focused on isolated drill and practice that may have contributed to his ongoing frustration with reading. The year Bradford was in my class, intervention services were limited to what I could provide in the classroom. His mother's interactions with schools have been tenuous, with school personnel tending to make assumptions about Ms. Holt and her family.

Within this complex dynamic of home and school, Bradford is in the process of developing his own identity as a reader. He is learning the mainstream discourses that surround learning to read yet also becoming aware of the ways these discourses fail to account for the lived experiences of members of his family. Where will Bradford's position be within this contextualized model of reading that has been presented in this book? Will his experiences allow him to invest in mainstream discourses about reading and education? Or will the tensions between mainstream and alternative discourses complicate his future understandings about the role of reading and schooling in his life? Figure 8.1 captures Bradford's dilemma. While his family and peers are positioned to the left side of the diagram, school staff are positioned to the right.

Alternative discourses that position schools as adversarial to families and the goals that children struggle to achieve are perhaps best exemplified in the following story of Bradford's oldest living brother, who was pushed out of school during May of his senior year despite, as reported by his mother, his being on the honor role during the previous semester. In the following section, an added complexity, the relative presence and absence of capital, will be explored in terms of Bradford's family.

BRADFORD'S FAMILY AND CAPITAL

Pierre Bourdieu's (1986) discussion of the various forms of capital enlightens discussions of the challenges that Ms. Holt and her children face. As described in Chapter 1, Bourdieu recognizes three forms of capital: economic capital, cultural capital, and social capital. Cultural capital can assume three states: embodied capital, objectified capital and institutional capital. Embodied capital refers to the mannerisms and social practices that people possess. Although Ms. Holt and her children have acquired various skills and abilities that include reading, they do not consistently

Figure 8.1. Bradford's Position

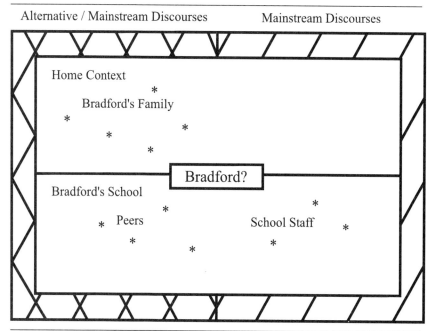

Alternative / Mainstream Discourses   Mainstream Discourses

Home Context
                    *
        Bradford's Family
    *
            *   *
                *
            *
                        Bradford?
Bradford's School
                            *
    *   Peers   School Staff   *
        *   *
            *

exhibit the narrow range of mannerisms and social practices that are valued and accepted within mainstream institutions due to the reluctance of these institutions to accept variations in speech, dress, and deportment.

While Ms. Holt possesses a high school diploma as well as a restaurant management certificate, her children lack academic certificates or other forms of institutional capital. Her daughter dropped out of school. Her son was pushed out of high school near the end of his senior year. While her son may possess the skills and abilities that were taught in his vocational education program, he lacks the institutional capital (diploma, certification, license) needed to legitimize his knowledge; Ms. Holt is particularly vexed at his being denied the diploma, reducing his chance of getting a good job.

> He made the honor role the last semester. Ms. Lilly, how you going to make honor role one, one semester [and] the next semester they tell him you're not going to graduate? . . . Then a few weeks before graduation, and we're prepping him for graduation, they're prepping him so he can go into [a vocation]. That's why he had

this um, this job things [a special class designed to help students transition to the world of work] to show him how you go to work. . . . Then when you're going through this you're going to turn around and tell me you're not going to graduate.

Objectified capital includes possessions of value that can be exchanged for economic capital. Visits to the Holt's home reveal no evident forms of objectified capital. Cooking is a valuable skill that Ms. Holt was able to transfer into institutional and economic capital as she pursued her certificate in restaurant management and attained employment. However, her son has neither material evidence of his accomplishments in trade school (objectified capital) nor a certificate (institutional capital) to legitimize his accomplishments.

In addition to the forms of cultural capital described above, economic capital and social capital also privilege individuals. With Ms. Holt fluctuating between part-time employment and unemployment, the Holt family does not possess substantial amounts of economic capital. Social capital is a more complex issue and refers to people's access to socially valued resources. Ms. Holt describes contacting the president of the school board, who was a good friend of her older brother as he was growing up.

I said my son doing this [getting pushed out of school] and whatever [he had been] going to school. He said, "I can't do anything" because he works with the neighborhood. . . . Yeah he's said "I'll look into this." But if he was, I know that they keep him so busy, but I'm going to find out [what's going on with my son]. I'm a, I'm gonna have him look into this.

Despite her intention to continue to work through the school board president, Ms. Holt does not appear confident that he will be able to help. As she explains, "They keep him so busy." Ms. Holt has adequate social capital to gain access to the president of the school board, but it is highly questionable whether her efforts will bear results. Perhaps her low status as a poor, African American single mother is reflected in the school board president's contradictory and evasive responses: he claims, "I can't do anything," while simultaneously responding, "I'll look into this." According to a later interview with Ms. Holt, this school board member never did follow through.

On another occasion Ms. Holt described what happened when a well-established nationally affiliated charitable organization set up a summer program in her neighborhood. Her children were denied entry into the program although she had filled out her application as soon as she had received it. She explained that the people who ran the program had filled the program up with the children of family members and friends who did not live in the neighborhood. As she explains, "This is my neighborhood. Where'd these kids right here live at? You're busing these kids, bringing these kids here. We live here. Why can't my child go here? This is my community!" Ms. Holt was told to raise the issue with her councilman, which she did. She describes the conversation.

> "Well Ms. Holt, I don't understand. I'll work [on this]; see what we can do." "Hey! My kids still aren't in camp, so what! You ain't doing anything. You're defeating my purpose." And [the name of the organization] gives them [funds] where's the money at? All ya'll ride in those big old pretty cars and ya'll get paid well. And then they even stop the summer lunch program.

Again Ms. Holt's efforts to exercise social capital are negated. I am unaware of social capital possessed by Ms. Holt's children.

As Luke (1996) describes, capital must be institutionally legitimated and acknowledged by people with power before an individual can benefit from possession of that capital. While Ms. Holt and her children possess the ability to read, in the case of her older son, this capital is likely to remain unrecognized within mainstream society because of her son's lack of economic, cultural, and social capital. Although Ms. Holt possesses some forms of institutional capital (her high school diploma and certificate in restaurant management), these are not highly valued within the larger society. Transferring her skills into capital that is recognized within the larger society (opening her own restaurant, attaining a high-paying position in restaurant management) would probably require forms of economic, cultural, and social capital that Ms. Holt does not possess.

So what are the possibilities for educational, economic, objectified, and institutional success for Ms. Holt and her family? What options are available that will enable Ms. Holt and her family to attain forms of cultural capital that can lead to occupational options for her children?

Ms. Holt obviously understands the ways in which the school system has acted upon her son, beginning with his placement in special education and ending with his being pushed out of school near the close of his senior year. The school system has denied her son opportunities to attain embodied, institutional, and objectified capital that could be converted into economic and social capital. Ms. Holt is aware that her son has been denied the promise of public education and reflects on the consequences that this situation could have in the lives of her younger children. However, being able to describe the situation is not enough. When her son is pushed out of school, Ms. Holt finds that both mainstream discourses that associate the ability to read with a diploma and alternative discourses that cite racism and structural inequities fail to present a means for dealing with the difficulties faced by her son. While Ms. Holt continues to identify learning to read as critical to her younger children's success, she faces the reality that learning to read alone was not the salve for her older children.

Freire (1986) and others (Delpit, 1995; Fairclough, 1989, 1993, 1995; Freire & Macedo, 1987; McLaren, 1988; Shor, 1992) recommend deconstructing the commonsense understanding of the world and revealing the means by which oppression operates. According to this argument, critical examination of oppression undertaken by groups of individuals can lead to social change. Ms. Holt, however, is already aware of the inequities that have defined life for her family; she understands how the school has contributed to the difficulties faced by her children. She recognizes that mainstream discourses do not reflect the experiences of her family. She is aware of the tension between what is and what was promised. I suggest that Ms. Holt has already deconstructed existing commonsense understandings of the world and participated in the construction of alternative discourses and understandings of the world. Nevertheless, she does not have confidence in the critique she has constructed nor a means for sharing these understandings with others within mainstream dominated society. While this tension may lead to frustration as people recognize the situations they are in and the constraints that surround them, these tensions are also a site of possibility. It is through exploring these tensions that researchers, educators, parents, and children can begin to conceptualize actions that can lead to increased opportunity and equity.

However, assumptions made about poor, African American single mothers and the accompanying stigma, along with mainstream discourses that define Ms. Holt's difficulties as personal failings (parental incompetence, innate deficiencies, and the inadequacy intimated by the special education status of her son) contribute to the continued dominance of mainstream discourses and the continued difficulties that Ms. Holt and her family face.

Ms. Holt's story demonstrates how reading is contextualized within a larger system that advocates that children learn to read but simultaneously negates their abilities and belittles their accomplishments. Her story challenges mainstream discourses that associate school success and eventual occupational success with the ability to read. Ms. Holt offers a myriad of alternative discourses that complicate the realization of possibilities for her children. Despite the tremendous challenges she faces, Ms. Holt refuses to give up or allow her children to lose faith in their abilities. "That's what

I tell Bradford about his reading. He can do it! 'Mommy I can't.' 'Why?' 'Because.' 'Because what?' 'You're not trying?' 'Because I can't.' 'But you're not telling me why you can't.'" Ms. Holt refuses to give up with Bradford and refuses to accept failure for her other children.

The words of my students and their parents demonstrate that reading develops within the social contexts of home and school and emphasizes the importance of local cultural practices that define reading within a particular community. The contextualized model of reading that has been constructed in this book contains a recognition of the social, economic, and political factors that affect the role of reading in people's lives, relationships that form around reading, and people's identities as readers. Inherent in this model is an acknowledgment of the role of factors outside the classroom that affect how my first-grade students and their parents construct their conceptualizations about reading. This contextualized model of reading recognizes both the role of people's life experiences and the ways in which social, economic, and political contexts affect people's concepts about reading.

IMPLICATIONS OF THIS RESEARCH

This research has several theoretical implications for expanding existing conceptions of reading:

- Concepts about reading must be recognized as social constructions grounded in people's own experiences, local cultural practices, and the social, economic, and political contexts in which people live. Each of these factors interact in complex and dynamic ways as people construct concepts about reading in their lives. This research suggests that the influence of family is particularly strong.
- The data collected suggests the need for acknowledging and examining a broad range of factors that relate to reading. In this study, concepts about reading were ingrained in family histories (spanning up to four generations); employment opportunities; the communities in which people live; the schools they attend; educational experiences of family members; the relationships between parents, teachers, students, and siblings; and the long-terms goals and dreams of families and individuals. In this book, we have only begun to explore the wide range of factors that affect people's concepts about reading.
- Educators and researchers must continually question assumptions about urban families and reading. This research demonstrates the importance of learning to read in the lives of poor urban families. When

researchers and educators begin to see beyond their assumptions, the actions of urban parents can be understood as rational and reasonable responses to the situations in which they live.

- There is a great need for much more teacher research that moves beyond examination of classroom practices and pedagogy. Many more teacher-researchers must begin to explore the larger contexts in which children live and learn in order to provide instructional experiences that are responsive to and supportive of the children we teach and their families.

- This research demonstrates the need to recognize and become respon-sive to how mainstream discourses and alternative discourses about reading affect the manner in which people make sense of reading and learning to read. While all discourses are ideological constructions bon-ded to particular social and political agendas, mainstream discourses in particular must be recognized as being connected with dominant power structures in our society. Furthermore, the tensions and contra-dictions that people experience as they try to reconcile their own reading experiences with mainstream discourses about reading must be ac-knowledged and respected.

- All the factors described here come together within a particular local context. Within poor urban communities assumptions about families, limited amounts of capital, a limited range of types of capital, and the dominance of mainstream discourses over alternative discourses grounded in the experiences of poor urban people severely restrict the possibility that large numbers of urban families will be able to achieve their goals of access to better jobs, better neighborhoods, better schools, and more equitable and humane living conditions.

- Finally, the tensions between competing discourses suggest the possibil-ity of change. These data suggest that the families of my students have developed an awareness of the ways in which they are positioned within the larger society. However, there is a critical need for communities to conceptualize actions that can lead to increased opportunity and equity. Research and dialogue need to occur within a "third space" (Gutierrez et al., 1999) created at the intersection of home and school.

While the model of reading presented earlier does depict reading as a contextualized activity, there is still substantial work to be done. First, I have no reason to believe that the concepts about reading held in other local communities will coincide with those described by my students and their parents. Because this research points to the contextualized nature of concepts about reading, even in urban populations with similar demo-graphics, both similarity and difference must exist. Furthermore, this study only explores a few concepts about reading; the many rich narratives and the range of topics discussed by participants suggest that there are many other important concepts about reading that have yet to be identified and explored. Finally, and perhaps most significant, once people's concepts about reading are explored in their complex and tension-laden essence, teachers can begin to build on the concepts that children and parents bring to the school door. Questions of what a contextualized model of reading means in terms of pedagogical practices need to be addressed.

Now the question becomes, What do these contradictions and the existence of "lines of tension" mean to me as a teacher? Beyond the writing of this book and articles, and the frustrating conversations I regularly have with some of my colleagues, how do the words of the parents of my students inform my role as the teacher of their children? I would like to present four possibilities.

First, I must resist judging the parents of my students. Prior to completing the research presented on these pages, I did not realize that the parents of my students were passionate about reading. I did not know that David's mother loves to read American history or that Alisa's mother trades novels with her friends. I would not have imagined Javon's and Tiffany's mothers staying up late at night to read. I must assume the best of parents even when initial impressions might suggest otherwise. I cannot assume that I know what other people's lives are like based on what I think I know about a particular family or community.

Second, I must strive to involve parents in my classroom but not as pawns helping me to accomplish my own agenda or to complete menial tasks. I must seek opportunities for parents to contribute what they have to offer. In the past, I have had students survey their parents about their reading habits and the role that reading plays in their lives. During a recent study of civil rights, parents and grandparents of my students came to school to describe their experiences during the civil rights movement; in many cases the parents and grandparents of my students are among the unsung heroes of that movement. Their firsthand accounts were powerful. When we studied occupations, we were able, through a small grant, to provide each child with a single-use camera, which their parents brought to work to capture themselves "on the job." These pictures were used to create books and became material for discussion during the unit. I must continue to create spaces in my instructional program to feature contributions of parents. All parents have a range of experiences that can contribute greatly to classroom learning.

The third possibility deals with teacher knowledge and awareness. As teachers, we need to become more knowledgeable about the ways that language and discourses operate in classrooms, schools, and society.

In the conclusion of his book *Language and Power*, Fairclough (1989) recommends the development of critical language awareness on the part of teachers and students. This awareness helps teachers to understand how the English language functions socially and politically. Fairclough maintains that this understanding has the potential to inform teaching and learning by inviting teachers, and students, to critically examine mainstream discourses as socially mediated ways of viewing the world that are ideologically laden. Teachers must recognize the dominance of mainstream discourses and how these discourses define and limit our attitudes about our students and their families. Teachers need to consider the possibility that alternative discourses have much to contribute to our understandings of urban classrooms and communities.

Finally, the relationships between teachers and families must change. How can we get to know parents in collegial relationships that deny the subject positionings that often occur within the teacher-parent dyad? This positioning is often exaggerated when the social class of the teacher is "above" that of the parents. Genuine conversations in which the parent's voice is heard and respected are desperately needed to counteract the effects of mainstream discourses. Currently, the alternative discourses of my students' parents are not heard or acknowledged by educators and policy makers. Instead, these alternative discourses are ignored, dismissed, and rejected; they are viewed as rationalizations intended to disguise the personal failings of families.

One unanticipated result of this research was that toward the conclusion of the project, two of the parents I worked with spontaneously thanked me for inspiring them to spend more time and effort in helping their child learn to read and in changing their own reading habits. Although during interviews, I refrained from making suggestions to parents about how I felt they should help their children and did not entertain any notions of changing the participating families, some parents reported that simply by talking with me about reading changed the ways they interacted with their children around reading.

As I entered Bradford's home for the third interview, Ms. Holt greeted me at the door and excitedly began to describe the ways our conversations have changed her reading habits:

> Me and Bradford we get there and we sit together and we read
> these books together. I hadn't been doing that. . . . I'm so proud of
> myself, 'cause I was wasn't doing that before. You know that every Saturday and Sunday I read the paper. . . . I normally just turn
> the news on and see what goes on, but now I pull the paper out.

Ms. Webster makes a similar claim: She explains that my working with Tiffany changed her reading relationship with Tiffany: "I'm going to tell you the truth . . . not until you started working with her and then I started with her. But it took you, you changed me." Perhaps in some way these interviews created a third space in which learning occurred for all of us.

Despite these apparent successes, advocating change in teacher-parent relationships is a deceptively simple solution, and there are serious limits to the effectiveness of individual teacher change. Redefining parent-teacher relationships will require educators to reexamine the discourses that they use to describe their school world. It involves more than changing opinions and ideas. Changing the relationship between teachers and parents means that teachers, including myself, must share responsibility for the success and failure of our students not only in terms of the pedagogies and materials we use in the classroom, but also in terms of our social responsibilities within the larger community. What will we as a society tolerate and allow for the children who live in poor urban areas and attend urban schools? Not only must we change the discourses of schools, we must also challenge the discourses of society.

As an urban teacher, I find that it is easy to get caught up in discourses that sensationalize the experience of teaching in an urban school. When I tell people where I teach, they are generally impressed. They comment on how difficult my job must be and how dedicated a teacher I am to work with "those kids." They ask if I am frightened by working in "that neighborhood," and there is always an opportunity for me to tell horror stories about my students and the school. As I tell these stories I attain the status of both a martyr and a hero. While it is tempting to buy into this discourse and fulfill the social expectations of those who think they know urban schools, perhaps it would be better to comment on our successful students, our involved parents, and the joys that accompany being a teacher of talented, capable students. Unfortunately, negative conversations too often occur in our staff rooms as teachers swap stories about their students and their students' families, with each story more terrible than the one before. We must not allow discourses of degradation and dismissal to pervade our schools and communities.

The parents I interviewed in this study are confident that learning to read is important for their children. They believe that reading will help their children to "get somewhere" in terms of a job, physical mobility, and imaginatively through the pages of a book. On the basis of my years of classroom teaching, I venture to suggest that both teachers and parents agree that learning to read is important; however, teachers and parents do not share an understanding of the complexities that affect learning to read and the supposed relationship between learning to read and economic success. While many educators continue to blame children and their families for the difficulties their students face, interviews with parents reveal a range of possibilities that point to the social and political complexities that accompany living in poor urban areas.

What would happen in my school if teachers learned more about the families of our students? How can teachers move beyond traditional parent-teacher conferences in which the teacher identifies each of the students' weaknesses and provides the parents with advice on how they can help? How can teachers refuse the role of expert as parents become informants rather than recipients of information? How can we create a third space in which the established social positionings of parent and teacher can be re-created in ways that allow teachers to recognize and become responsive to the alternative discourses that parents bring?

As educators we must continue to work toward revealing alternative discourses and developing ways of sharing these alternative interpretations. It is my hope that this book, the words of my students, and the words of their parents will contribute to this goal.

While definitive answers cannot be claimed, the words of my students and their parents help us to begin to understand the ways in which urban parents and students conceptualize the purpose of reading and how one learns to read. These conceptions about reading reflect not only the social, economic, and political contexts in which people live, but also mainstream discourses and alternative discourses about reading.

The discourses my participants adopt and adapt to describe their concepts about reading are ideologically laden. Recognizing the social and ideological nature of discourses provides teachers and researchers with ways of viewing the words of parents and students as products of their lived experiences situated within social, economic, and political contexts.

Most significant are the ways in which these constructed concepts about reading affect the lived experiences of children and their parents. People's conceptions about reading influence how parents and children identify themselves as readers and the social relationships that accompany reading and learning to read. Conceptions about reading point to assumed relationships between reading, employment, and social position, often leaving urban residents disillusioned and without recourse when such relationships fail. Through the stories they tell and the discourses they adopt, parents and students demonstrate how their conceptions about reading and learning to read are products of their reading experiences both at home and at school and are subject to the influences of both mainstream and alternative discourses.

Appendix

Table A1. Gender, Ethnicity, and Age Information of Students

Name	Gender	Ethnicity	Age-related information
Alisa*	F	African American	
Nadine	F	Hispanic American	
Allen	M	African American	
Ariana	F	African American	
Bradford*	M	African American	Attended prefirst
Christy*	F	African American/ European American	Repeating Grade 1
Clarence	M	African American	
David*	M	African American/ European American	
Devin	M	African American	
Devon	M	African American	Repeating Grade 1
Diamond	F	African American	
Gabriella	F	Hispanic American	
Jacon	M	African American	
James	M	African American	
Jasmine*	F	Hispanic American	
Javon*	M	African American	
Jermaine*	M	African American	
Jerome	M	African American	
Jesse	M	African American	

(continued)

Table A1. *(continued)*

Name	Gender	Ethnicity	Age-related information
Lamar	M	African American	
Lashanda	F	African American	
Lecara	F	African American	
Leron	M	African American	
Marvin*	M	African American	
Peter*	M	African American	
Roshawn	M	African American	
Seana	F	African American	
Shawanda	F	African American	
Thomas	M	African American	
Tiffany*	F	Hispanic American/ European American	

All children without a comment on age were 6 years old.

* Denotes a "focus child."

Table A2. Gender, Ethnicity, and Age of Parents

Name	Gender	Ethnicity	Age
Ms. Green	F	European American	41
Ms. Hernandez	F	Hispanic	24
Ms. Horner	F	African American	26
Ms. Hudson	F	African American	42
Mr. Sherwood*	M	African American	49
Ms. Holt	F	African American	44
Ms. Mason	F	African American	37
Ms. Rodriguez	F	African American	34
Ms. Johnson	F	European American	35
Ms. Webster	F	European American	29

* Mr. Sherwood is actually Marvin's stepgrandfather; he and Marvin's grandmother have primary responsibility for Marvin.

Table A3. Family Overviews

Parent/Child	Gender	Age	Employment	Education	Family
Ms. Green	F	41	None	Associate's degree	Single
Christy	F	7			
Ms. Hernandez	F	24	None	Did not graduate	Married
Jasmine	F	6			
Ms. Horner	F	26	Phone company	GED	Single
Peter	M	6			
Ms. Hudson	F	42	None	Did not graduate, home/health certificate	Married
Jermaine	M	6			
Mr. Sherwood*	M	49	Maintenance	Graduated high school and trade school	Married
Marvin	M	7			
Ms. Holt	F	44	Food service	Graduated high school	Single
Bradford	M	6			
Ms. Mason	F	37	Preschool	Graduated high school	Single
Javon	M	6			
Ms. Rodriguez	F	34	Preschool	GED, child care certificate	Married
Alicia	F	6			
Ms. Johnson	F	35	Food service	GED, business school	Married
David	M	6			
Ms. Webster	F	29	Secretarial	Graduated high school, computer/job training classes	Single
Tiffany	F	6			

* Mr. Sherwood is actually Marvin's stepgrandfather; he and Marvin's grandmother have primary responsibility for Marvin.

References

Adams, M. J. (1990). *Beginning to Read: Thinking and Learning About Print.* Cambridge, MA: MIT Press.

Apple, M. (1979). *Ideology and Curriculum.* Boston: Routledge & Kegan Paul.

Apple, M. (1996). *Cultural Politics and Education.* New York: Teachers College Press.

Apple, M., & Christian-Smith, L. (Eds.). (1991). *The Politics of the Textbook.* New York: Routledge.

Ashton, P. T. (1986). *Making a Difference: Teachers' Sense of Efficacy and Standard Achievement.* New York: Longman.

Bakhtin, M. M. (1981). Discourse in the Novel. In M. Holquist (Ed.), *The Dialogic Imagination: Four Essays by M. M. Bakhtin* pp. 259–422. Austin: University of Texas.

Bakhtin, M. M. (1986). The Problem of Speech Genres. In C. Emerson & M. Holquist (Eds.), *Speech Genres and Other Late Essays* (pp. 60–102). Austin: University of Texas.

Bartoli, J. S. (1995). *Unequal Opportunity-Learning to Read in the U.S.A.* New York: Teachers College Press.

Barton, D., & Hamilton, M. (1998). *Local Literacies: Reading and Writing in One Community.* London: Routledge.

Belle, D. (Ed.). (1982). *Lives in Stress.* Beverly Hills, CA: Sage.

Block, A. A. (2000). Resisting Occupation, Resisting Reading. *Language Arts, 78*(2), 129–137.

Bloome, D. (1985). Reading as a Social Process. *Language Arts, 62*(2), 134–142.

Bourdieu, P. (1986). The Forms of Capital. In J. G. Richardson (Ed.), *Handbook of Theory and Research for the Sociology of Education* (pp. 241–258). New York: Greenwood Press.

Brodkey, L. (2000). Writing on Bias. In L. Weis & M. Fine (Eds.), *Construction Sites: Excavating Race, Class, and Gender Among Urban Youth* (pp. 5–25). New York: Teachers College Press.

Bruner, J. (1986). *Actual Minds, Possible Worlds.* Cambridge, MA: Harvard University Press.

Burawoy, M. (1991). *Ethnography Unbound: Power and Resistance in the Modern Metropolis.* Los Angeles: University of California Press.

Cairney, T., & Ruge, J. (1997). *Community Literacy Practices and Schooling* [Electronic database]. (2001). Queensland, Australia: Griffith University.

Carney, S. (2000). Body Work on Ice. in L. Weis & M. Fine (Eds.), *Construction Sites: Excavating Race, Class, and Gender Among Urban Youth* (pp. 121–139). New York: Teachers College Press.

Chall, J., Jacobs, V., & Baldwin, L. (1990). *The Reading Crisis: Why Poor Children Fail.* Cambridge, MA: Harvard University Press.

Clay, M. (1991). *Becoming Literate: The Construction of Inner Control.* Portsmouth, NH: Heinemann.

Clay, M. (1993). *An Observation Survey of Early Literacy Achievement.* Portsmouth, NH: Heinemann.

Clay, M. (1996). Forward. In S. McNaughton (Ed.), *Patterns of Emergent Literacy: Processes of Development and Transition* (pp. ix–x). Melbourne, Australia: Oxford University Press.

Cochran-Smith, M. (2000). Blind Vision: Unlearning Racism in Teacher Education. *Harvard Educational Review, 70*(2), 152–190.

Delpit, L. (1995). *Other People's Children: Cultural Conflict in the Classroom.* New York: The New Press.

Dyson, A. H. (1993). *Social Worlds of Children Learning to Write in an Urban Primary School.* New York: Teachers College Press.

Dyson, A. H. (1997). *Writing Superheros: Contemporary Childhood, Popular Culture, and Classroom Literacy.* New York: Teachers College Press.

Fairclough, N. (1989). *Language and Power.* New York: Longman.

Fairclough, N. (1993). *Discourse and Social Change.* Cambridge, MA: Polity Press.

Fairclough, N. (1995). *Critical Discourse Analysis.* New York: Longman.

Fendler, L. (1998). What Is It Impossible to Think? A Genealogy of the Educated Subject. In T. Popkewitz & M. Brennan (Eds.), *Foucault's Challenge: Discourse, Knowledge, and Power in Education* (pp. 39–63). New York: Teachers College Press.

Fine, M. (1991). *Framing Dropouts: Notes on the Politics of an Urban High School.* New York: State University of New York Press.

Fine, M. (1993). (Ap)parent Involvement: Reflections on Parents, Power, and Urban Public Schools. *Teachers College Record, 94*(4), 683–729.

Fine, M., & Weis, L. (1998). *The Unknown City: The Lives of Poor and Working-Class Young Adults.* Boston, MA: Beacon Press.

Fingeret, A. (1982a). *The Illiterate Underclass: Demythologizing an America Stigma.* Unpublished doctoral dissertation, Syracuse University, New York.

Fingeret, A. (1982b). *Through the Looking Glass: Literacy as Perceived by Illiterate Adults.* Paper presented at the American Educational Research Association, New York.

Fingeret, A., & Drennon, C. (1997). *Literacy for Life: Adult Learners, New Practices.* New York: Teachers College Press.

Frank, C. (1999). *Ethnographic Eyes: A Teacher's Guide to Classroom Observation.* Portsmouth, NH: Heinemann.

Freire, P. (1986). *Pedagogy of the Oppressed.* New York: Continuum.

Freire, P., & Macedo, D. (1987). *Literacy: Reading the Word and the World.* South Hadley, MA: Bergin and Garvey.

Gee, J. P. (1990). *Social Linguistics and Literacies: Ideology in Discourses.* London: Falmer Press.

Gee, J. P. (1992). *The Social Mind: Language, Ideology and Social Practice.* New York: Bergin and Garvey.

Giroux, H. (1992). *Border Crossings: Cultural Workers and the Politics of Education.* New York: Routledge.

Giroux, H., & McLaren, P. (1994). *Between Borders: Pedagogy and the Politics of Cultural Studies.* New York: Routledge.

Goodman, K. (1996). *On Reading.* Portsmouth, NH: Heinemann.

Gordon, B. (1993). Black Aesthetic: Reconstructing Classroom Pedagogy as Alternative Narratives for Teachers and Students. *Theory into Practice, 32*(4), 219–226.

Gore, J. (1993). *The Struggle for Pedagogies: Critical and Feminist Discourses as Regimes of Truth.* New York: Routledge.

Graff, H. (1979). *The Literacy Myth: Literacy and Social Structure in the Nineteenth-Century City.* New York: Academic Press.

Grumet, M. (1988). *Bitter Milk: Women and Teaching.* Amherst, MA: University of Massachusetts Press.

Gutierrez, K., Baquedano-Lopez, P., & Tejeda, C. (1999). Rethinking Diversity: Hybridity and Hybrid Language Practices in the Third Space. *Mind, Culture, and Activity, 6*(4), 286–303.

Heath, S. B. (1983). *Ways With Words: Language, Life, and Work in Communities and Classrooms.* Cambridge: Cambridge University Press.

Hill, S., Comber, B., Louden, W., Rivalland, J., & Reid, J.-A. (1998). *100 Children Go to School* [Electronic database]. (2001). Queensland, Australia: Griffith University.

Hymes, D. (1996). *Ethnography, Linguistics, Narrative Inequality: Toward an Understanding of Voice.* London: Taylor & Francis.

Kohl, H. (1994). *"I Won't Learn from You" and Other Thoughts on Creative Maladjustment.* New York: The New Press.

Kunjufu, J. (1986). *Developing Positive Self-Images and Discipline in Black Children.* Chicago: African American Images.

Ladson-Billings, G. (1994). *The Dreamkeepers: Successful Teachers of African American Children.* San Francisco: Josey-Bass.

Lawrence-Lightfoot, S. (1978). *Worlds Apart: Relationships Between Families and Schools.* New York: Basic Books.

Lemert, C., & Branaman, A. (1997). *The Goffman Reader.* Malden, MA: Blackwell.

Lieblich, A., Turval-Mashiach, R., & Zibler, T. (1998). *Narrative Research: Reading, Analysis, and Interpretation.* Thousand Oaks, CA: Sage.

Luke, A. (1995a). Getting Our Hands Dirty: Provisional Politics in Post Modern Conditions. In R. Smith & P. Wexler (Eds.), *After Postmodernism: Education, Politics, and Identity* (pp. 83–97). Washington, DC.: Falmer Press.

Luke, A. (1995b). Text and Discourse in Education: An Introduction to Critical Discourse Analysis. In M. Apple (Ed.), *Review of Research in Education* (Vol. 21) (pp. 3–47). Washington DC.: American Educational Research Association.

Luke, A. (1996). Genres of Power? Literacy Education and the Production of Capital. In R. Hasan & G. Williams (Eds.), *Literacy in Society* (pp. 308–338). New York: Longman.

Luke, A., & Freebody, P. (1997). Shaping the Social Practices of Reading. In S. Muspratt, A. Luke, & P. Freebody (Eds.), *Constructing Critical Literacies: Teaching and Learning Textual Practices* (pp. 185–225). Cresskill, NJ: Hampton Press.

Madigan, D., & Koivu-Rybicki, V. T. (1997). *The Writing Lives of Children.* York, ME: Stenhouse.

May, J. P. (1995). *Children's Literature and Critical Theory.* New York: Oxford University Press.

McCormick, K. (1994). *The Culture of Reading and the Teaching of English.* New York: Manchester University Press.

McLaren, P. (1988). Culture or Cannon? Critical Pedagogy and the Politics of Literacy. *Harvard Educational Review, 58*(2), 213–234.

McLaren, P. (1989). *Life in Schools.* New York: Longman.

Mehan, H. (1992). Understanding Inequality in Schools: The Contributions of Interpretive Studies. *Sociology of Education, 65*(1), 1–20.

Moll, L. C., Amanti, C., Neff, D., & Gonzalez, N. (1992). Funds of Knowledge for Teaching: Using a Qualitative Approach to Connect Homes and Classrooms. *Theory Into Practice, 31*(2), 132–141.

Morris, P. (1994). *The Bakhtin Reader: Selected Writings of Bakhtin, Medvedev, Voloshinov.* London: Arnold.

New London Group. (1996). A Pedagogy of Multiliteracies: Designing Social Futures. *Harvard Educational Review, 66*(1), 60–92.

Nieto, S. (1996). *Affirming Diversity: The Sociopolitical Context of Multicultural Education.* White Plains, NY: Longman.

Noddings, N. (1992). *The Challenge to Care in Schools: An Alternative Approach to Education.* New York: Teachers College Press.

Pinnell, G. S., & Fountas, I. (1996). *Guided Reading: Good First Teaching For All Children.* Portsmouth, NH: Heinemann.

Purcell-Gates, V. (1995). *Other People's Worlds: The Cycle of Low Literacy.* Cambridge, MA: Harvard University Press.

Rhodes, L. K., & Shanklin, N. L. (1993). *Windows into Literacy: Assessing Learners, K–8.* Portsmouth, NH: Heinemann.

Seal, K. (2000, September 12). Does Your Child Need a Tutor? What's Helpful and What's Not. *Family Circle,* 66–70.

Shannon, P. (1998). *Reading Poverty.* Portsmouth, NH: Heinemann.

Shannon, P. (2001). *iSHOP You Shop.* Portsmouth, NH: Heinemann.

Shockley, B., Michalove, B., & Allen, J. B. (1995). *Engaging Families: Connecting Home and School Literacy Communities.* Portsmouth, NH: Heinemann.

Shor, I. (1992). *Empowering Education: Critical Teaching for Social Change.* Chicago: University of Chicago Press.

Strauss, A., & Corbin, J. (1990). *The Basics of Qualitative Research: Grounded Theory Procedures and Techniques.* Newbury Park, CA: Sage.

Street, B. (1995). *Social Literacies: Critical Approaches to Literacy in Development, Ethnography, and Education.* New York: Longman.

Taylor, D. (1983). *Family Literacy: Children Learning to Read and Write.* Portsmouth, NH: Heinemann.

Taylor, D. (1991). *Learning Denied.* Portsmouth, NH: Heinemann.

Taylor, D. (1996). *Toxic Literacies: Exposing the Injustice of Bureaucratic Texts.* Portsmouth, NH: Heinemann.

Taylor, D., & Dorsey-Gaines, C. (1988). *Growing Up Literate: Learning from Inner-City Families.* Portsmouth, NH: Heinemann.

Voloshinov, V. N. (1973). *Marxism and the Philosophy of Language.* (L. Matejka, Trans.). New York: Seminar Press.

Voloshinov, V. N. (1983). Literary Stylistics. In A. Shukman (Ed.), *Bakhtin School Papers: Russian Poetics in Translation, vol. 10* (pp. 93–152). Oxford, UK: RPT Publications and Holdan Books Ltd.

Weaver, C. (1994). *Reading Process and Practice* (2nd ed.). Portsmouth, NH: Heinemann.

Weis, L. (1992). Reflections on the Researcher in a Multicultural Environment. In C. Grant (Ed.), *Research and Multicultural Education: From the Margins to the Mainstream* (pp. 47–57). London: Falmer Press.

Wertsch, J. (1990). The Voice of Rationality in a Sociocultural Approach to Mind. In L. C. Moll (Ed.), *Vygotsky and Education: Instructional Implications and Applications of Sociohistorical Psychology* (pp. 111–126). Cambridge, MA: Cambridge University Press.

Willis, A., & Harris, V. (2000). Political Acts: Literacy, Learning and Teaching. *Reading Research Quarterly, 35*(1), 72–88.

Winters, W. G. (1993). *African American Mothers and Urban Students: The Power of Participation.* New York: Lexington Books.

Index

About the Author

Catherine Compton-Lilly is a first-grade and Reading Recovery teacher in Rochester, New York, and a visiting associate professor at Saint John Fisher College. She has taught in the public schools of New York State since 1985. Catherine Compton-Lilly received her Ed.D. in Curriculum and Human Development from the University of Rochester in 2000. She has written several articles and book reviews and serves on the editorial board of *Networks*, a teacher research Internet journal. Dr. Compton-Lilly has recently been awarded a National Academy of Education/Spencer Postdoctoral Fellowship to continue her research in literacy, urban education, and diversity.